OUR CHOICE

AL GORE

OUR CHOICE

How We Can Solve the Climate Crisis

MELCHER
MEDIA

PUFFIN BOOKS
An Imprint of Penguin Group (USA) Inc.

RODALE
LIVE YOUR WHOLE LIFE

PUFFIN BOOKS

Published by the Penguin Group
Penguin Young Readers Group,
345 Hudson Street, New York, New York 10014, U.S.A.
Penguin Group (Canada), 90 Eglinton Avenue East,
Suite 700, Toronto, Ontario, Canada M4P 2Y3
(a division of Pearson Penguin Canada Inc.)
Penguin Books Ltd, 80 Strand,
London WC2R 0RL, England
Penguin Ireland, 25 St Stephen's Green,
Dublin 2, Ireland (a division of Penguin Books Ltd)
Penguin Group (Australia), 250 Camberwell Road,
Camberwell, Victoria 3124, Australia (a division of
Pearson Australia Group Pty Ltd)
Penguin Books India Pvt Ltd, 11 Community Centre,
Panchsheel Park, New Delhi - 110 017, India
Penguin Group (NZ), 67 Apollo Drive, Rosedale,
North Shore 0632, New Zealand (a division of Pearson
New Zealand Ltd)
Penguin Books (South Africa) (Pty) Ltd, 24 Sturdee
Avenue, Rosebank, Johannesburg 2196, South Africa

Registered Offices:
Penguin Books Ltd,
80 Strand, London WC2R 0RL
England

Published simultaneously by Puffin Books and Viking
Children's Books, divisions of Penguin Young Readers
Group, 2009, in agreement with Rodale, Inc., 733 3rd
Avenue, New York, New York 10017.

Text adapted by Richie Chevat

This book was produced by

 MELCHER
MEDIA

124 West 13th Street
New York, NY 10011
www.melcher.com

Publisher: Charles Melcher
Associate Publisher: Bonnie Eldon
Editor in Chief: Duncan Bock
Project Editor: Megan Worman
Production Director: Kurt Andrews
Production Associate: Daniel del Valle

Book design by karlssonwilker, inc.

10 9 8 7 6 5 4 3 2 1

LIBRARY OF CONGRESS DATA IS AVAILABLE
ISBN 978-0-14-240981-7

Printed in the United States of America

The publisher does not have any control over and does
not assume any responsibility for author or third-party
websites or their content.

The author and publisher have made extensive efforts
to ensure the accuracy of the information contained in
this book. Any errors brought to the attention of the
author or publisher will be corrected in future editions.

TO WYATT, ANNA, AND OSCAR

CONTENTS

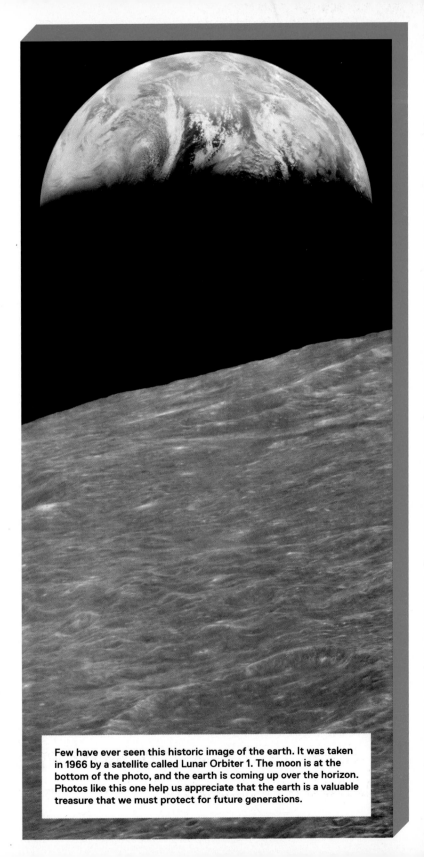

Few have ever seen this historic image of the earth. It was taken in 1966 by a satellite called Lunar Orbiter 1. The moon is at the bottom of the photo, and the earth is coming up over the horizon. Photos like this one help us appreciate that the earth is a valuable treasure that we must protect for future generations.

INTRODUCTION

In 2006, I published a book called *An Inconvenient Truth,* which was also a film with the same title. Both the movie and the book explained some frightening facts: the earth's climate is getting warmer; human beings are causing this global warming; and unless we do something, this change will destroy our way of life.

These are tough things to think about. It's especially tough for young people to think about growing up in a world with so many problems.

When *An Inconvenient Truth* came out, many people did not know about global warming, even though most scientists in the world agreed that it was happening. But as the years have passed by since then, even more evidence has been found by the scientists. Today, most Americans not only understand that global warming is real but want to do something about it.

That's what this book is about. It's about the things we can do, the things we *must* do, to stop global warming before it's too late.

For the past three years, I have met with many scientists, engineers, and climate experts. What I have learned

from them has given me hope. Most of them say we still have time, if we act right away, to head off the worst effects of global warming.

It won't be easy. It will take years to turn things around. But we already have all of the knowledge and technology we need. We have the tools we need to save our planet, but we must choose to use them. That's why this book is called *Our Choice.* It's about the choice we must make if future generations are to keep living on our home, the earth.

GOING FAR, QUICKLY

There is an old African proverb that says:

"If you want to go quickly, go alone; if you want to go far, go together."

To solve the climate crisis, we have to go far...quickly. There is a lot to do, and we must begin now. I wrote this book to explain, step-by-step, as clearly as I could, exactly what we

Penguins returning to their breeding place on Deception Island, Antarctica.

must do. I wanted to gather in one place all of the solutions to the climate crisis. And I wanted to make it absolutely clear that these solutions are all possible. These ideas are not science fiction—the science and technology we need exist today.

I hope that this young readers edition inspires you to take action. Many young people ask me, "What can I do to help fight global warming?" The answer is that we must act together—in our communities, our schools, as a nation, and around the whole world. There is no way that something as big as the climate crisis can be fixed only by individuals acting alone. It can only be solved by all of us acting together.

Yes, we have to change the lightbulbs in our houses to use less electricity. Yes, we have to find ways to get around without burning so much gasoline in cars. Yes, we all have to recycle more. These individual solutions are important, and they all add up. But they're just the beginning.

To solve the climate crisis, we must change the way our entire society works. Among other things, we have to change the way we get our energy, the way we use energy, and the way we grow our food. To make those changes, we have to change our laws, we have to change the way we do business, and we have to change the way we think.

What can young people do? Throughout history, young people have led the way in fighting for change. Young people are more open to new ideas, and they aren't afraid to try things that seem hard or even impossible. In the 1950s and '60s, during the Civil Rights movement, it was often young people who stood up for what was right. By their example, they showed adults that a new way of doing things was possible. They helped change a nation, and they made history.

I believe that young people today can play an important role in the movement to stop global warming. Everywhere I go, I find young people who are already doing this. They are teaching others about global warming, or writing petitions to their local governments, or raising money for environmental groups. Even if they aren't old enough to vote, they are changing minds and influencing politicians. This is exactly the kind of activism we will need to turn around our country and our world.

CHANGING THE WORLD

To get at the roots of the climate crisis, we must stop using carbon-based fossil fuels like oil and coal. We have to switch to renewable energy sources like solar and wind power. But

Indian schoolchildren take part in a mass tree-planting drive in Hyderabad in 2008.

switching to renewable energy will do more than head off the climate crisis. New ways of making and getting energy will make it easier for poor nations to develop their economies. This will make it easier to fight poverty, disease, and hunger.

And that brings me to another thing I have learned over the past few years. The climate crisis is connected to all of the other big problems we face. The only way to solve the climate crisis is for the people of the world to work together. We must all learn to act responsibly—toward each other and toward our planet. We must learn to live in balance with the natural world. We must be able to have open, free discussions in a democratic way, free from the influence of money and power.

If we do these things, we will do more than save our environment. We will lay the foundation for a more peaceful, just, and humane world. If all that sounds like an awful lot to accomplish, it is. Yet I believe we can do it, and the reason is simple: either we make these changes or we face the destruction caused by global warming. That fact should help people to make the hard choices that are necessary. Any other decision is unthinkable.

A MOMENT IN HISTORY

We have arrived at a moment unlike any other in all of human history. Our home is in grave danger. Of course, we cannot destroy the earth itself, but we can make it impossible for future human beings to live on it.

The novelist Kurt Vonnegut once imagined what would happen "if flying-saucer creatures or angels or whatever were to come here in a hundred years, say, and find us gone like the dinosaurs."

Vonnegut tried to think of a good message for humanity to leave for those visitors, maybe carved in great big letters on a wall of the Grand Canyon. What he came up with went something like this:

We probably could have saved ourselves, but we were too lazy to try very hard, and too cheap.

This idea might make you laugh (or it might make you cry). But in the end, I don't think that's what is going to happen. I think the human race, faced with this terrible crisis, will rise to the occasion. I think once people have all the facts, they will make the right choice.

There are many obstacles in front of us. There are people who, for their own reasons, will try to stop humanity from making that choice. I talk about that in the pages of this book and explain what we can do to make sure we succeed. The main thing to remember is that we can solve the climate crisis. It will be hard, to be sure, but if we choose to solve it, I have no doubt whatsoever that we can and will succeed.

And as we set out to solve this crisis, we should take pride in what we are doing. Those of us alive today have a rare privilege that few generations in history have known. We have a historic mission. We know that if we do our job, if we make the hard choices, young people in the future will look back and thank us for leaving them a world worth growing up in.

THEY WILL THANK US FOR MAKING THE RIGHT CHOICE.

One thin September soon
A floating continent disappears
In midnight sun

Vapors rise as
Fever settles on an acid sea
Neptune's bones dissolve

Snow glides from the mountain
Ice fathers floods for a season
A hard rain comes quickly

Then dirt is parched
Kindling is placed in the forest
For the lightning's celebration

Unknown creatures
Take their leave, unmourned
Horsemen ready their stirrups

Passion seeks heroes and friends
The bell of the city
On the hill is rung

The shepherd cries
The hour of choosing has arrived
Here are your tools

—Al Gore, Nashville, Tennessee, 2009

The Niederaussem coal-fired power plant in Germany is the second worst emitter of carbon dioxide in Europe.

CHAPTER 1

WHAT GOES UP MUST COME DOWN

Climate change, global warming, climate crisis—it has different names, but they all mean the same thing: the earth's environment is changing, and we, human beings, are the primary cause.

The way that we live our lives is hurting the earth's ecological system. The factories that produce our computers and televisions, the planes we fly, and the cars we drive all put toxic chemicals—pollution—into the air and water. We cut down forests and destroy coral reefs. We spoil and waste precious resources like the topsoil where we grow our crops or the stocks of fish in the oceans. We destroy the homes of animals, their *habitats*. We give no thought to where future generations will get their food or energy or clean water.

15

All of these things, caused by human activity, add up to a very serious ecological crisis. But out of all these problems, the most serious is the climate crisis.

The climate crisis affects every corner of the globe. It threatens our farms, our food, our towns and cities, the way we work, and the way we live. Not only that, but the climate crisis is at the root of many of our other environmental problems. If we don't do something about it, and fast, it could forever change the way human beings live on this planet.

There's a lot of science that goes into explaining the climate crisis, but the basic idea is very simple:

Human beings are putting pollution into the atmosphere. That pollution is trapping heat and raising the temperature of the air, the oceans, and the surface of the earth.

We know exactly which kinds of air pollution are causing global warming. (There are six major types.) We know where and how they are made. We know how to stop creating them. And so the solution to global warming is simple: we have to sharply cut back on the global warming pollution that we put in the air.

It's simple, but that doesn't make it easy. . . .

You know the saying "What goes up must come down?" Well, that's true for global warming pollution. It goes up into the sky, but it also comes down, some of it quickly and some very slowly. To fight the climate crisis, we have to reduce the amount that goes up and increase the amount that comes down.

That's what this book is about—reducing what goes up and increasing what comes down. "Our Choice" means just that—we have a choice to make, and we have to make it right now. We can prevent the worst and make it possible for future generations to enjoy the planet, but only if we take action today.

What Goes Up Comes Down—But How Fast?

DOWN

UP

Global warming pollution goes up into the sky. Sooner or later it does come down, but not fast enough to stop global warming. To fight the climate crisis, we have to greatly reduce the amount of pollution we put into the air.

SIX TYPES OF GLOBAL WARMING POLLUTION

These six types of pollution are the main causes of global warming. Five are gases that are normally found in the air, but human beings are creating more and more of these gases. This is changing the balance of the atmosphere and causing global warming. (Black carbon is not a gas, but soot—tiny pieces of carbon waste. We are adding this to the air too.)

This chart shows how much each type of pollution adds to global warming. Carbon dioxide is the worst, causing 43 percent of global warming.

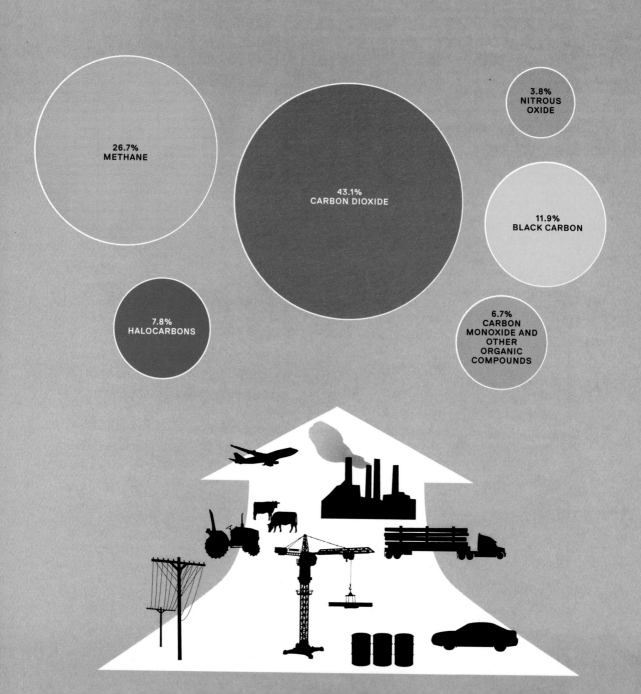

26.7%
METHANE

43.1%
CARBON DIOXIDE

3.8%
NITROUS OXIDE

11.9%
BLACK CARBON

7.8%
HALOCARBONS

6.7%
CARBON MONOXIDE AND OTHER ORGANIC COMPOUNDS

THE SIX CAUSES OF GLOBAL WARMING

There are six types of air pollution, created by human beings, that together are causing the climate crisis. They are:

1. CARBON DIOXIDE

The gas carbon dioxide (CO_2) is by far the biggest cause of global warming. It may seem strange to talk about carbon dioxide pollution. After all, it's a natural part of our atmosphere. In fact, CO_2 and other greenhouse gases are the reason the earth is warm enough to support life. The problem is that we are adding huge amounts of CO_2 to the air, and this is making the earth warmer.

Carbon dioxide is not just the biggest cause of global warming, it is also the fastest-growing cause. Every time you burn anything, you release carbon dioxide into the atmosphere.

The single biggest source of CO_2 is the burning of fossil fuels: oil, coal, and gas. These are called fossil fuels because they really are fossils—hundreds of millions of years ago, they were trees, plants, and tiny life-forms in the ocean that took carbon from the atmosphere. When the plants died, many wound up buried deep underground. Over millions of years, the buried plant life changed into oil, natural gas, and coal.

Today, human beings are digging up those plant fossils and burning them, releasing all that carbon back into the atmosphere.

We burn gasoline and other oil-based fuels in our cars, trucks, and airplanes. We burn coal to produce electricity. We burn gas and oil to heat our homes and run our factories. That's why one way to end the climate crisis is to find new sources of energy. Wind and solar power, for example, produce electricity without producing carbon dioxide.

Industrial countries, like the United States, the nations of Europe, and China, burn most of the fossil fuels in the world. But a lot of CO_2 pollution comes from less developed countries. In many places in the world where people live by farming, they burn large areas of forest to create farmland. They also clear their farmland every year by burning what remains of their crops. Those fires release huge amounts of CO_2. To end the climate crisis, we have to find solutions that include all countries—both industrial and less developed.

SOURCES OF GLOBAL WARMING POLLUTION

COAL MINING

INDUSTRIAL PROCESSES

MELTING PERMAFROST

COAL PLANTS

INDUSTRIAL AGRICULTURE

The pollution that is causing global warming comes from human activity. Carbon dioxide is produced whenever we burn something. When we burn coal to make electricity, when we burn gasoline in our cars, or when we burn gas in our stoves, we add more carbon dioxide to the air. Methane is produced by hundreds of millions of cows and other livestock as well as by rice paddies. It also escapes from waste in landfills and from leaks in natural gas pipelines. Black carbon is soot, tiny pieces of carbon in the air. It comes from burning forests and grasslands. These are just a few of the ways we are changing the atmosphere and destroying our climate.

FERTILIZATION

CROP BURNING

LAND TRANSPORTATION

OIL PRODUCTION

LANDFILLS

FOREST BURNING

▶▶ **There's good news and bad news about CO_2. Here's the good news: if we stopped putting excess CO_2 into the atmosphere tomorrow, about half of the man-made CO_2 would fall to the earth within 30 years.**

Here's the bad news: As much as 20 percent of the CO_2 we put in the air this year will stay there for 1,000 years. And we're putting 90 million tons of CO_2 into the atmosphere every single day!

The good news means there is still time to act. If we start cutting CO_2 right away, we might be able to avoid the most harmful results of global warming. The bad news means that we haven't started acting yet, and there is no time to waste.

➡ THE GREENHOUSE EFFECT

Carbon dioxide and methane are two greenhouse gases. They are called that because they trap heat coming up from the earth, a little bit like the way a glass roof traps heat inside a greenhouse.

Energy from the sun, in the form of

sunlight, enters the earth's atmosphere and strikes the surface of the planet. Then some of that energy bounces back into space in the form of heat (infrared radiation). CO_2 and other greenhouse gases absorb the infrared radiation, trapping the heat in the atmosphere.

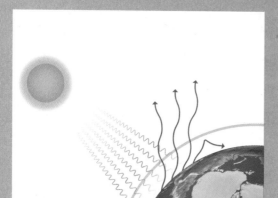

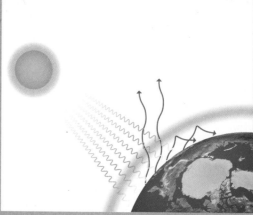

2. METHANE

The second biggest cause of the climate crisis is methane. Like CO_2, methane occurs naturally. Natural gas, the kind burned in kitchen stoves, is mainly methane. But just as we are with CO_2, we are adding large amounts of methane into the atmosphere.

We put less methane into the air than CO_2. But over time, methane is much more powerful at trapping heat than carbon dioxide is. That makes methane a big source of global warming.

A major source of methane is livestock—cows, pigs, and chickens. These animals produce methane when they digest plants. For example, there are about 1.5 billion cows in the world, and they all produce methane. (Most of it comes out when cows belch, but some of it comes out the other end.)

Another source of methane is permafrost, the frozen soil in the Arctic. This soil has been frozen for thousands of years, but now, thanks to global warming, it's beginning to melt. In the permafrost are huge amounts of plant matter. As these plants thaw out and decay, they release methane.

If the permafrost continues to melt, then huge amounts of methane will go into the atmosphere. The methane will add to global warming and cause more permafrost to melt, which will release more methane, and on and on. This is another reason we have to act quickly, before the climate crisis gets out of control.

There is some good news about methane. Natural gas is something people depend on to heat their homes, and refineries make their money by creating natural gas. A lot of the methane that goes into the air comes from leaks in natural gas pipes and refineries. The more the refineries can stop the leaks or sell methane that has leaked from other sources (like landfills), the higher their profits. (See Chapter 6 to learn more about this.)

3. BLACK CARBON

Black carbon, or soot (tiny pieces of carbon floating in the air), is the third biggest source of the climate crisis. Black carbon is not a greenhouse gas like carbon dioxide or methane. It doesn't trap heat coming up from the earth. Instead, it absorbs heat from incoming sunlight as it enters the atmosphere.

The largest source of black carbon is the burning of forests and grasslands. This is a big problem in Brazil, Indonesia, and the countries of Central Africa. People in those areas are burning forests to make room for farms (sometimes to raise cows, which, as we've discussed, produce methane). Forest fires are also a big source of black carbon. Still more comes from the burning of wood, coal, and even cow dung to heat homes. It also comes out of the tailpipes of trucks, cars, and buses that run on diesel fuel.

Large clouds filled with black carbon cover vast areas of Europe and Asia. The clouds float over the Pacific Ocean and across the Indian Ocean. Black carbon usually does not stay in the atmosphere for long, because it is washed out of the air by rain. However, every day we replace it with new soot from fires.

CLEANING UP THE GREAT SMOG OF 1952

The "fogs" that used to cover London were really mostly smoke and soot. The smog came from the coal fires in factories and homes. In December 1952, a terrible smog descended over London for five dark days, killing 4,000 people. From this disaster came swift action to improve the country's air quality. In 1956, Parliament introduced the Clean Air Act, which outlawed the burning of coal in open-hearth fires. It encouraged replacement of coal with cleaner sources of energy, such as gas, oil, and electricity. As a result, smog is no longer a part of London life. This is a good example of how government action can protect and restore the environment. Now we need government action to end global warming.

A SHINY PROBLEM

A full moon is very bright, but it does not have any light of its own. Moonlight is just reflected sunlight. In the same way, if you saw the earth from space, it would also shine with reflected sunlight. The ability of the earth to reflect sunlight (and heat) is an important part of our climate.

You may have learned in science class that dark things absorb heat and light things reflect heat. That's very important to the climate of the earth. The large white polar ice caps reflect heat from the sun back into space. (See picture 1.) The glaciers that cover the Himalayas and other mountain ranges also reflect heat.

Unfortunately, when black carbon falls out of the sky, it can still add to global warming. When it falls on ice and snow, they stop reflecting sunlight. Instead, the soot absorbs heat. This causes the ice to melt. Of course, if the ice melts, there is even less of it to reflect light and heat back into space. (See pictures 2–4.) Because of black carbon and the melting of the ice caps, the earth is losing its natural ability to reflect sunlight. This could make the problem of global warming much harder to solve.

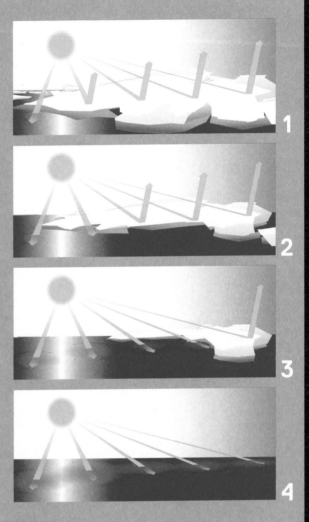

Albedo: The Scale of Shine Scientists use the word *albedo* to describe how well something reflects sunlight. An object that has an albedo of zero percent is black. An object that has an albedo of 100 percent is white. You can see that snow and ice have high albedos and reflect a lot of sunlight (and heat). As we lose our ice caps and glaciers, the earth does not reflect as much heat. This adds to global warming.

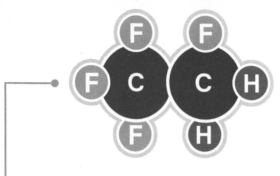

4. HALOCARBONS

The fourth biggest cause of global warming is a group of chemicals called halocarbons. Halocarbons called CFCs (chlorofluorocarbons) were once used in hair spray and air conditioners. These chemicals became big news in the 1980s when it was discovered that they were eating a hole in the ozone layer. The ozone layer is a part of our atmosphere that keeps harmful radiation from hitting the earth. Without it, life on earth would not be possible.

In 1987, the governments of the world moved to protect the ozone. They signed a treaty, called the Montreal Protocol, that set limits on the amounts and types of halocarbons. As a result, this type of global warming pollution is slowly declining. Still, more needs to be done to cut halocarbons even further.

In some ways, the response to the ozone crisis was like the response to global warming. At first, many business leaders and politicians said there was no crisis. However, once the facts were proved, governments quickly came together to act. This shows that it is possible for the nations of the world to work together to solve big environmental problems.

5. CARBON MONOXIDE AND OTHER ORGANIC COMPOUNDS

The next cause of global warming is actually a group of chemicals that includes carbon monoxide. In the U.S., carbon monoxide mainly comes from car exhaust. In less developed countries, the main source of carbon monoxide is the burning of grass, trees, and other plant matter.

6. NITROUS OXIDE

The last major cause of global warming is nitrous oxide. The largest amount of the nitrous oxide we add to the air comes from the use of artificial (man-made) fertilizer. Like carbon, nitrogen is one of the basic elements plants need to build cells. But too much nitrous oxide is bad for the environment.

One hundred years ago, there was no such thing as artificial fertilizer. To make crops grow, farmers used manure from animals. They also planted crops that add nitrogen to the soil, like soybeans. Today, modern factory farms use tons of artificial fertilizer to add nitrogen to their fields. This makes it easier to grow large amounts of grain and other crops. However, these huge amounts of artificial fertilizer create several types of pollution.

First, making fertilizer in a factory burns large amounts of fossil fuels, which, as we know, releases CO_2 and causes global warming. Adding the fertilizer to farmland releases nitrous oxide, which also causes global warming. Finally, large amounts of extra fertilizer run into streams and rivers, causing even more environmental problems.

Nitrous oxide plays a small but significant role in the earth's warming. Yet it is a cause we can sharply reduce. For example, we can change the way we use nitrogen on our farms. That alone would be an important way to reduce global warming.

So there it is: The cause of global warming is easy to describe. So is the solution. There are six kinds of global warming pollution, and we have to sharply cut back on all of them. At the same time, we have to find ways to remove those pollutants from the air. (Remember, what goes up must come down.)

But of course, just because something is simple to describe doesn't mean it is easy to do. The hard part isn't figuring out what to cut or how. The hard part is getting people around the world to agree that it must be done. The hard part is getting people to see that we have a choice to make and we must make it—now.

A natural gas well off the coast of Thailand. Excess gas is burned off at many gas and oil wells. That's just a small part of the contributions fossil fuels make to global warming.

CHAPTER 2

WE NEED (CARBON-FREE) ENERGY

To solve the climate crisis, we have to find ways to get energy without releasing more carbon dioxide into the air.

When we burn gasoline in our cars, we're using energy. When we turn on an electric light, we're using energy. When we turn up the heat in our houses (or the air conditioner), we're using energy.

The modern world requires lots of energy. The problem is that most of the energy we use comes from the burning of fossil fuels—oil, coal, and gas. As we have seen, burning those fuels releases huge amounts of carbon dioxide into the atmosphere. That extra CO_2 is the biggest cause of global warming.

We already know how to produce energy without releasing CO_2. - - - - - -

Solar power, wind power, and geo-thermal power are all nearly carbon-free. If we choose, we can switch the world from global warming energy to carbon-free energy. Convincing people to make that choice is the hard part.

The single largest cause of global warming is the production of energy from fossil fuels. The most important solution to the climate crisis is to produce energy in ways that release little or no CO_2.

COAL AND STEAM

For most of human history, people burned wood for energy. Burning wood does not cause a rise in the level of CO_2 if new trees grow and take the carbon back out of the air. This cycle can go on—as long as people do not cut down too many trees.

But as the human population grew, so did the demand for firewood. Around A.D. 500, about 95 percent of Europe was covered with forests. But by the early 1600s, most of those forests were gone. People needed another source of fuel, so they turned to coal.

In the mid-1700s, the Industrial Revolution started in England. It was a time when machinery began to replace human and animal power. As part of this revolution, iron and steel production expanded. This increased the demand for coal even more, since metalworkers needed the high temperatures they could get from coal fires.

As the demand for coal grew, miners had to dig deeper into the earth for it. As the coal mines went deeper, they sometimes filled up with water. And so the steam engine was invented—to pump water out of coal mines.

Soon steam engines were being used everywhere. They replaced horses and pulled trains. They replaced farm workers and were used to harvest crops. They replaced wind power and moved steamships across the oceans. Steam engines replaced the windmill and the water mill. The energy to do all that work came from burning coal.

Today, coal and steam are still linked together. Almost half the electricity in the world comes from burning coal to produce steam. The force of the steam turns a giant turbine. A shaft from the turbine turns magnets in an electric generator. When the magnets spin inside a coil of wire—or a coil of wire spins inside a magnet—an electric current is produced. (See the diagram on page 33.)

HOW TURBINES MAKE ELECTRICITY

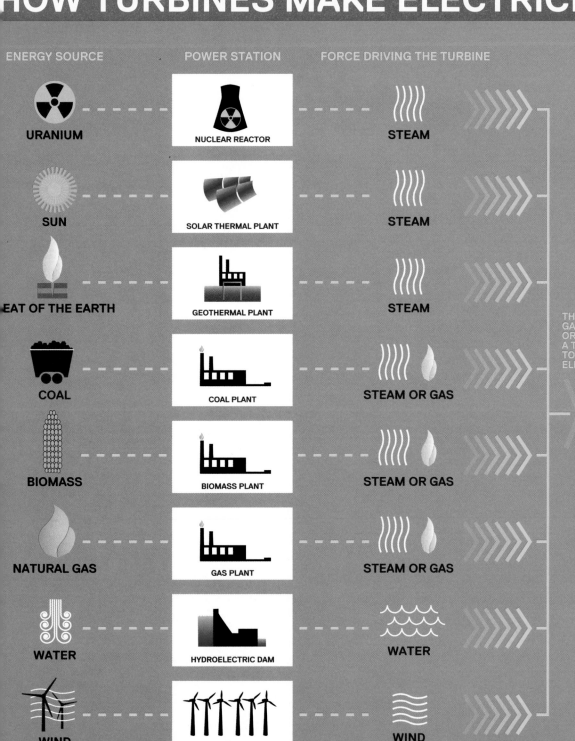

ENERGY SOURCE

POWER STATION

FORCE DRIVING THE TURBINE

URANIUM — NUCLEAR REACTOR — STEAM

SUN — SOLAR THERMAL PLANT — STEAM

EAT OF THE EARTH — GEOTHERMAL PLANT — STEAM

COAL — COAL PLANT — STEAM OR GAS

BIOMASS — BIOMASS PLANT — STEAM OR GAS

NATURAL GAS — GAS PLANT — STEAM OR GAS

WATER — HYDROELECTRIC DAM — WATER

WIND — WIND FARM — WIND

THE STEAM, GAS, WATER, OR WIND TURNS A TURBINE TO CREATE ELECTRICITY.

TURN THE PAGE FOR MORE!

HOW TURBINES MAKE ELECTRICITY

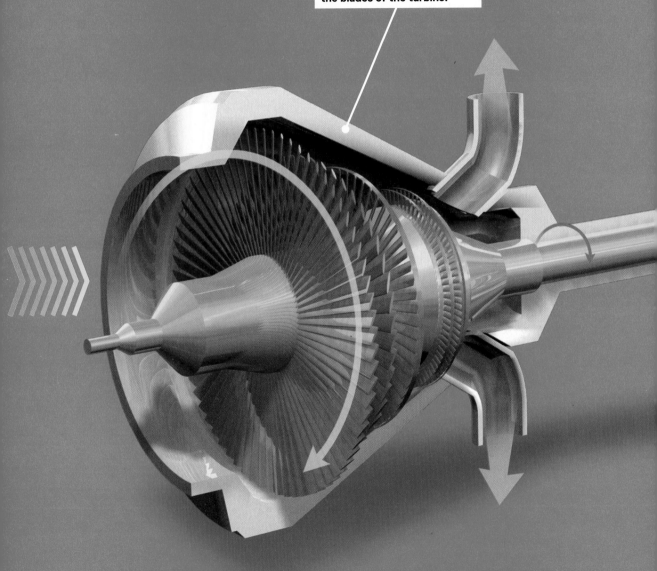

THE TURBINE

A turbine is like a large fan or windmill. The force of steam, hot gases, water, or wind spins the blades of the turbine.

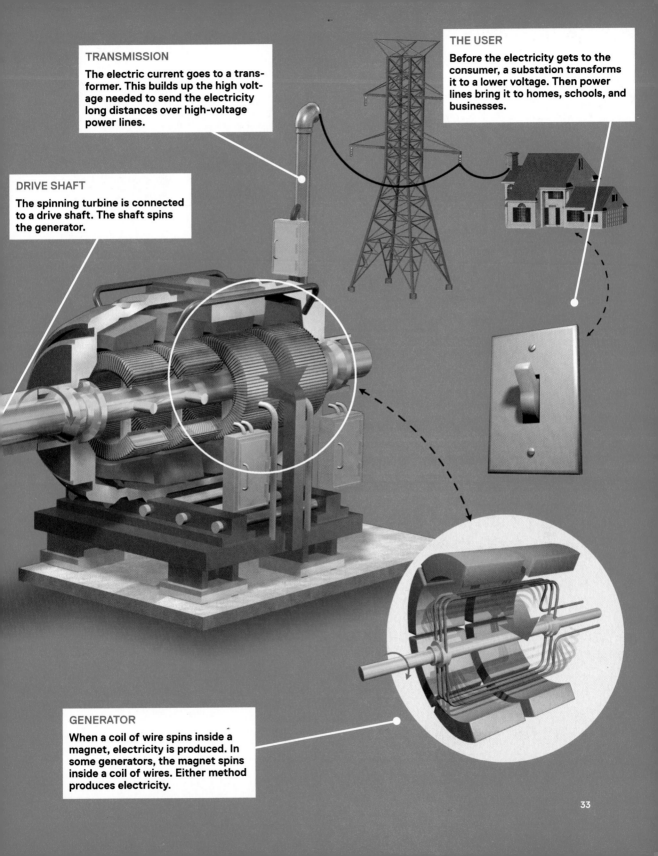

TRANSMISSION

The electric current goes to a transformer. This builds up the high voltage needed to send the electricity long distances over high-voltage power lines.

THE USER

Before the electricity gets to the consumer, a substation transforms it to a lower voltage. Then power lines bring it to homes, schools, and businesses.

DRIVE SHAFT

The spinning turbine is connected to a drive shaft. The shaft spins the generator.

GENERATOR

When a coil of wire spins inside a magnet, electricity is produced. In some generators, the magnet spins inside a coil of wires. Either method produces electricity.

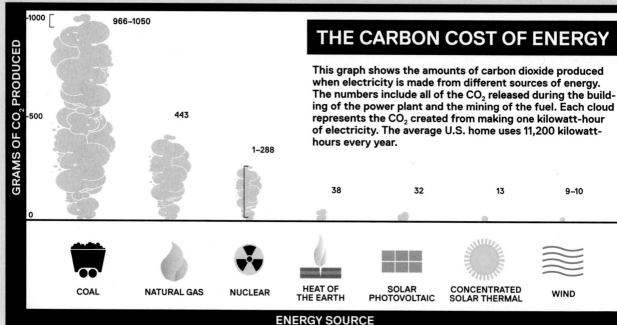

THE CARBON COST OF ENERGY

This graph shows the amounts of carbon dioxide produced when electricity is made from different sources of energy. The numbers include all of the CO_2 released during the building of the power plant and the mining of the fuel. Each cloud represents the CO_2 created from making one kilowatt-hour of electricity. The average U.S. home uses 11,200 kilowatt-hours every year.

GRAMS OF CO_2 PRODUCED

- 1000
- 500
- 0

966–1050

443

1–288

38

32

13

9–10

| COAL | NATURAL GAS | NUCLEAR | HEAT OF THE EARTH | SOLAR PHOTOVOLTAIC | CONCENTRATED SOLAR THERMAL | WIND |

ENERGY SOURCE

LIQUID ENERGY

Almost half of our electricity comes from coal, but coal is not the largest source of energy on the planet. The largest source of energy is oil, or petroleum. Gasoline, diesel fuel, heating oil, propane, and kerosene are just a few of the energy products made from oil.

More than half of the petroleum we use is burned in cars and trucks. Most of the rest is burned in engines to run machinery. Some oil is used as the raw material for all sorts of chemical products, like plastics and nylon. Less than 10 percent is used to heat homes, and less than 6 percent is used to make electricity.

Although the world depends on oil for energy, the largest amounts of oil are found in just a few countries. That means that most countries, including the United States, have to import oil from overseas. The biggest reserves of oil are found in the countries of the Middle East, where the struggle for oil has been one cause of wars and conflicts. So in addition to solving the climate crisis, there is another good reason to end our use of oil. We must choose to produce our energy at home instead of buying it overseas.

IS NATURAL GAS BETTER?

Natural gas is sometimes found in the same place as petroleum and sometimes found alone. It now provides about 23 percent of the world's energy. One third of all natural gas is burned to make electricity. It's also used for heat in homes and gas stoves.

All three fossil fuels—coal, oil, and gas—produce CO_2 when burned. But they produce different amounts of CO_2. Oil produces less CO_2 than coal. Natural gas is even better. It gives off only half the CO_2 of coal.

That's why some people say we should switch to natural gas while we look for new sources of energy. But the climate crisis is already too serious to do that for very long. Burning natural gas already produces almost 20 percent of CO_2 pollution. If we want to avoid the worst of the climate crisis, we have to cut all forms of CO_2 production—now.

WHERE'D YOU GET THAT ELECTRICITY?

Electricity is the fastest-growing type of energy on the planet. It powers our washing machines, our computers, our mp3 players, and, of course, our electric lights. We use it every day without even thinking about it.

But electricity, although it is a type of energy, is not a *source* of energy. We produce electricity from other types of energy. And that is the big problem. Say you want to help stop CO_2 pollution, so you buy an electric car. If you charge it with electricity produced from coal, you are still adding CO_2 to the air, even though none is coming out of your car. Your electric car will only help stop CO_2 pollution if you use carbon-free electricity. That's why we have to know where our electricity comes from.

In fact, more than 60 percent of our electricity comes from burning fossil fuels. The rest comes from sources that do not produce large amounts of CO_2. Hydroelectric dams provide almost 20 percent of our electric power. Another 15 percent comes from nuclear power. Right now a very small amount comes from solar, geothermal, and wind power. We have to increase those carbon-free sources as fast as we can.

CARBON-FREE RENEWABLE ENERGY

The exciting news is that there is basically an unlimited supply of low-CO_2 sources for electricity. If you added up the amount of energy the earth receives from the sun in just 50 days, it would equal the energy in all the fossil fuel in the world—including the stuff still in the ground. That's right—all the fossil fuel in the world equals less than two months of solar power. That means there's more than enough solar power hitting the earth to solve the climate crisis—if we choose to use it.

And sunlight is just one source. There's hydroelectric and wind and geothermal power (power that uses the heat deep within the earth). If we choose, we can completely replace CO_2-rich fossil fuels with these renewable sources of energy.

The energy is renewable because it comes from sources that will never be

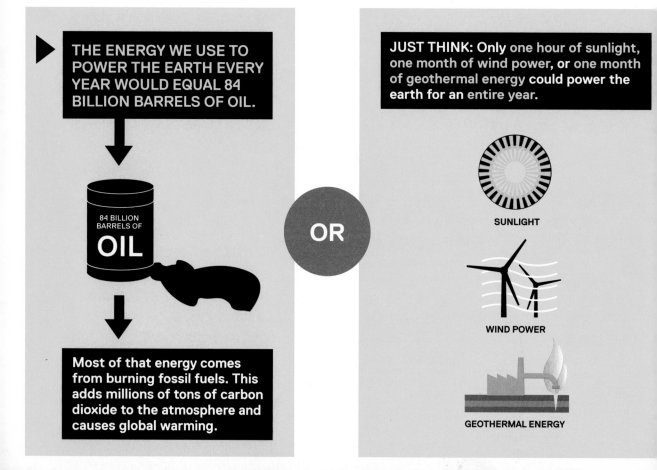

THE ENERGY WE USE TO POWER THE EARTH EVERY YEAR WOULD EQUAL 84 BILLION BARRELS OF OIL.

84 BILLION BARRELS OF OIL

Most of that energy comes from burning fossil fuels. This adds millions of tons of carbon dioxide to the atmosphere and causes global warming.

OR

JUST THINK: Only one hour of sunlight, one month of wind power, or one month of geothermal energy could power the earth for an entire year.

SUNLIGHT

WIND POWER

GEOTHERMAL ENERGY

> **" I'd put my money on the sun and solar energy. What a source of power! I hope we don't have to wait until oil and coal run out before we tackle that. "**
>
> —*Thomas Edison, 1931*

used up. The sun will keep shining (at least for a few billion years). The wind will keep blowing. There's no limit to it.

But before we can get that renewable energy, we do have to invest a lot of money. We have to improve solar, wind, and geothermal technology. We have to build a better electric grid to get electricity where we need it. We have to replace our fossil fuel–burning cars and trucks with new electric ones.

We know this can be done. When new inventions come on the market, like a new kind of television, digital camera, or cell phone, at first they are very expensive. As more people buy them and more companies rush to make them, their prices drop. The same thing is happening with renewable energy.

Solar panels and wind turbines are expensive now, but the costs will drop. We can help the costs to drop faster by getting the government to invest in research and development.

Where does your town get its electricity? Is it carbon-free? What about your school? We should get our towns to buy more carbon-free renewable energy. That will not only cut carbon pollution but it will help bring down the price of clean energy.

Once there is a growing market for solar and wind energy, companies and scientists will compete to make even better solar panels and wind turbines. Think of how computers and cell phones have gotten better in just the past few years. Now imagine what can be done for renewable energy.

We can have all the energy we need without destroying the planet. It's there for the taking—if we choose.

Giant curved mirrors concentrate the sun's energy at one of several solar-electric-generating plants in California's Mojave Desert. These plants can produce enough power for 230,000 homes.

CHAPTER 3

SOLAR POWER

We can produce all the electricity we need from our greatest source of energy—sunlight.

We know that there is plenty of renewable energy in the world. Much of it is in the form of solar power. There's more energy in two months of sunlight than in all the fossil fuel in the world.

In fact, the sun is the source of almost all energy on Earth. All living things get their energy from sunlight one way or another. Plants use sunlight to store energy in their roots, leaves, fruits, and seeds. Animals get solar energy by eating plants. Even fossil fuels got their energy from the sun, because fossil fuels started out as plants millions of years ago.

This "Power Tower" near Seville, Spain, uses mirrors to concentrate the sun's rays and create steam. This is just one type of solar power plant.

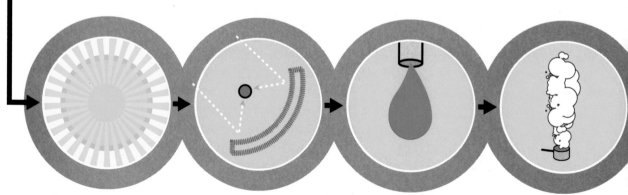

HOW CONCENTRATED SOLAR POWER WORKS

1. It all starts with sunlight.

2. Large mirrors focus sunlight on containers filled with water or other liquid.

3. The water or liquid is heated to several hundred degrees Fahrenheit.

4. Boiling the water makes steam.

-▶ The trick to solving the climate crisis is to get our power directly from the sun instead of fossil fuels. We already know how to do this. We just have to make the choice. Producing electricity from sunlight is one of the best ways to solve the climate crisis.

STEAM FROM THE SUN

Right now, about 40 percent of the world's electricity comes from burning coal. We burn coal to heat water and make steam. The power of the steam turns turbines, which power electric generators.

However, there is no reason that the heat to make steam has to come from burning coal. We can use the heat of sunlight to produce steam and generate electricity. Scientists have already invented ways to concentrate sunlight to produce enough heat to boil water.

This is called the *concentrated solar thermal* (CST) method.

There are quite a few CST power plants in operation around the world. They use very large mirrors to focus sunlight on pipes filled with water. The heat of the sunlight boils water and makes steam. (In some CST plants, there is an extra step. The sunlight is used to heat a special liquid, and then the heat in that liquid is used to boil water. Either way, the result is the same.)

These CST plants are like coal-fired plants in many ways—but they don't create carbon pollution. They can be connected to the same high-voltage wires that already bring electricity to your home. You can use the same TV, refrigerator, and other appliances you already own. And these carbon-free power plants can be built right now.

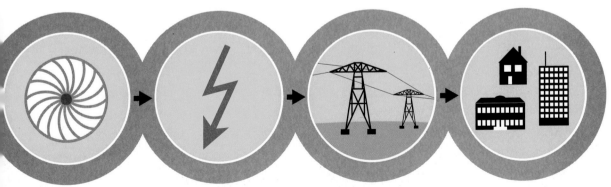

5. The force of the steam spins a turbine.

6. The turbine is connected to a generator that creates electricity.

7. The electricity is sent out over high-voltage power lines.

8. The electricity is used by consumers in homes, schools, and businesses.

VOLTS FROM THE SUN

Another way to produce electricity from sunlight is by using *photovoltaic* (PV) cells. (*Photo* is Greek for light. A *volt* is a unit of electricity. So photovoltaic = light electricity.)

You've probably seen shiny black solar panels on the roofs of homes and buildings. Those panels are made of photovoltaic cells, and they can turn sunlight directly into electricity. No steam or turbines are needed.

To understand how PV cells work, you have to know that an electric current is the movement of *electrons* through a wire. (Electrons are the particles that circle the nucleus of an atom.) Think of a wire as a tube full of marbles, except the marbles are electrons. Each electron bumps into the one in front of it, pushing it along.

Now imagine a ray of sunlight as a stream of tiny particles. These particles are called *photons*. Each time a photon hits a PV cell, it knocks an electron loose. A stream of photons (sunlight) creates a stream of electrons (electricity). That's how PV cells create electricity from sunlight.

YOUR VERY OWN POWER PLANT

The argument against photovoltaic cells has been that they cost too much. But that is quickly changing. PV cells are made of silicon, like the silicon chips in a computer or video game. As demand for PV cells has grown, more and more companies have begun making them. This is bringing the cost of the panels down. Like their cousins the computer chips, PV cells are getting cheaper and better all the time. It is possible that PV power will soon be cheaper than fossil fuel power.

Even today, some people are willing to spend a little more to get clean energy from the sun. That's why many businesses and homeowners have already put solar panels on their roofs. These home solar power plants make electricity whenever the sun is shining. In many places, if you don't use all the power, you can sell it to your local power company.

And of course, fossil fuel electricity is only cheaper now if you don't count the tremendous damage it's doing to our planet and our lives. The real cost of a coal-based power plant does not appear on your electric bill. It appears

HOW PHOTOVOLTAIC CELLS WORK

Photovoltaic cells use sunlight to make electricity. They can be put together in large groups, or *arrays*, to work as a power plant, or they can be put onto the roofs of buildings.

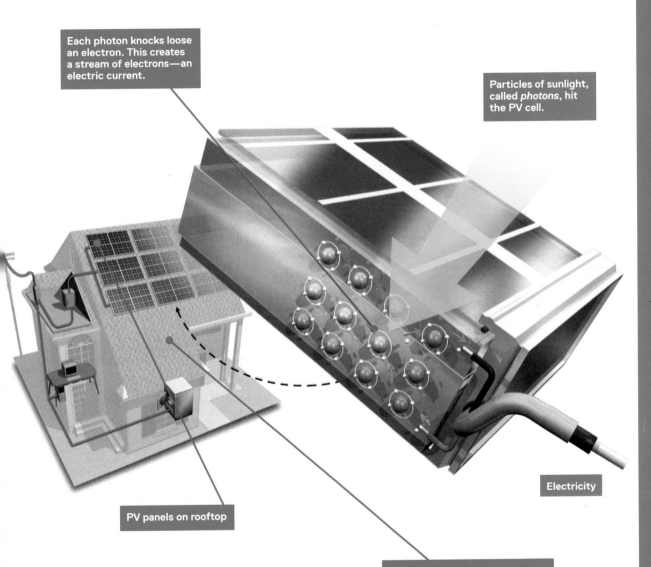

Each photon knocks loose an electron. This creates a stream of electrons—an electric current.

Particles of sunlight, called *photons*, hit the PV cell.

Electricity

PV panels on rooftop

PV panels or solar panels can supply electricity to a house or building. If the panels make more electricity than the homeowners need, they can sell the extra energy to their power company.

in the shrinking ice caps, the melting permafrost, and the changing climate of the earth. The cost of those changes will be very high, indeed.

A "SMART" GRID

One problem with solar power plants is that they only work when the sun is shining. At night, or when there's a thick cloud cover, they can't produce electricity. But this is not as big a problem as you might think. Different regions of the country are already linked by a nationwide power grid. We need to improve that grid to make it "smarter," using computer technology. This will allow us to shift electricity from places where the sun is shining to places where it is not.

Solar power can also be built in partnership with wind power. It turns out that sometimes, when the sun is not shining, the wind is blowing. So these two types of renewable energy can work side by side, supplying power day and night.

In addition, some of the energy produced by solar plants during the day can be stored for one hour (but soon to be five or six hours or even more) at night. For example, CST plants produce a lot of heat, some of which can be stored to make electricity when the sun is not shining. And if everyone drove electric cars, we could store power in millions of rechargeable car batteries.

At night, the electrical grids of Detroit, Michigan (top of photo), and Windsor, Ontario (bottom of photo), are clearly visible.

SPACE ELECTRICITY

There's one place where the sun is always shining and there are never any clouds—outer space. That's why some scientists have proposed building a power plant in outer space. The space plant would orbit the earth at a distance of 22,300 miles, with large banks of photovoltaic cells. The energy would then be sent back to Earth in a microwave beam. Is this kind of space-based electric plant possible? Would the microwave beam be safe? Most scientists today say yes. Would it cost too much to build? That question still has to be answered. But even if the idea doesn't work out, it shows that there are many ways to use solar energy still waiting to be explored.

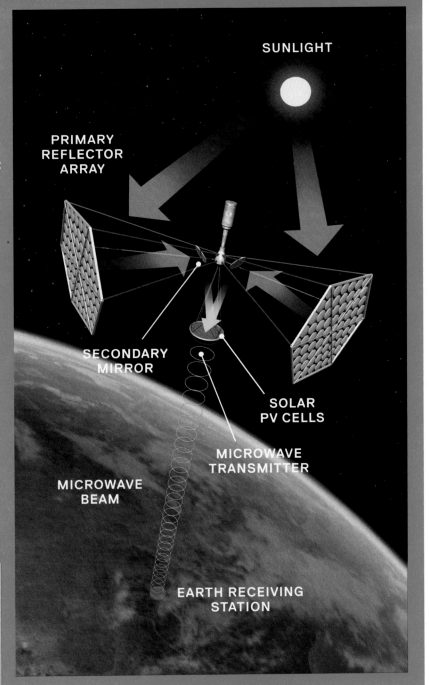

SUNLIGHT

PRIMARY REFLECTOR ARRAY

SECONDARY MIRROR

SOLAR PV CELLS

MICROWAVE TRANSMITTER

MICROWAVE BEAM

EARTH RECEIVING STATION

A PASSIVE SOLAR HOME

Here's another way to get energy from the sun. We can use the heat of sunlight directly.

Rooftop hot-water heaters use sunlight instead of fossil fuels to make hot water. Smart builders place windows so they get plenty of sunshine in the winter but not as much in the summer. Thick walls and insulation keep in heat and save your heating costs. They also keep heat out in the summer and save on air-conditioning. This kind of design is called *passive solar*. (Passive is the opposite of active. The design is passive because the house just has to sit there and let the sun do the work.) Passive solar design is a way average homeowners can lower their energy costs and help end our use of fossil fuels.

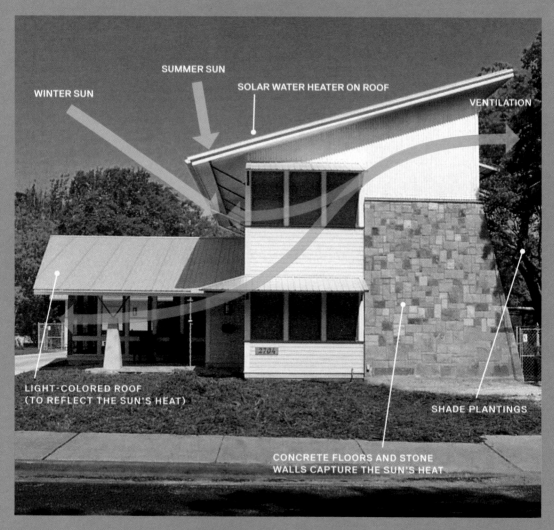

WINTER SUN

SUMMER SUN

SOLAR WATER HEATER ON ROOF

VENTILATION

LIGHT-COLORED ROOF
(TO REFLECT THE SUN'S HEAT)

SHADE PLANTINGS

CONCRETE FLOORS AND STONE
WALLS CAPTURE THE SUN'S HEAT

SOLAR POWER, NOW

Solar power is not a new idea. The first photovoltaic cell was created at Bell Labs in New Jersey in 1954. Nine concentrated solar thermal power plants were built in the Mojave Desert of Southern California in the 1980s. They have been producing electricity for 25 years. If we had followed their example, the whole country would now be using a lot more solar power.

Yet our government has not given steady support to solar energy. This is for two reasons: First, there is more public support for solar power when oil and gas prices rise, but as soon as prices fall, some people forget about the need for clean, renewable energy. Second, oil and coal companies, as well as coal-burning electric companies, spend hundreds of millions of dollars to influence public opinion. They have worked hard to stop our government from spending the money needed to develop solar power.

In other countries, such as Germany and Spain, government has strongly supported the growth of solar power. This has brought down the price and encouraged the invention of new solar systems. China and Taiwan are racing to become the world leaders in photovoltaic technology. Meanwhile, only one of the world's biggest PV manufacturers is in the U.S.

Other governments see that solar power means millions of new, high-paying jobs for their people. We could be doing the same thing here in the United States.

The good news is that this is beginning to change. In the past 10 years, new and improved CST plants have been built in Arizona and Nevada. Many more are now being planned. New laws in some states force utilities to buy some of their electricity from renewable sources. A new photovoltaic plant is being built in Florida.

But this is just the beginning, and we must move much faster. There is no question that in the future, solar power will provide much of our electricity. Will that happen in time to solve the climate crisis? Only if we choose.

Wind turbines on a farm in Sherman County, Oregon.

CHAPTER 4

WIND POWER

Wind power is another way we can produce large amounts of clean electricity.

We see the power of the wind all the time. When a sailboat moves across the water, when a kite flies, when a windmill turns, we are seeing the wind at work. The power of the wind can also help solve the climate crisis if we put it to work making electricity. There is enough wind power in the world to provide five times our total energy needs.

Wind power is the fastest-growing form of renewable energy. In fact, it is the fastest-growing source of any form of energy. In 2007, more wind power was added in the United States than coal, gas, and nuclear power combined.

The technology for making electricity from wind power already exists. We know how to build wind turbines and where to place them. We are already getting electricity from wind farms. To help solve the climate crisis, all we have to do is choose to build more.

WIND POWER = SOLAR POWER

Remember we said that almost all of the energy on Earth comes from the sun? Well, wind power is really another form of solar energy, and it can work alongside solar power to solve the climate crisis.

Winds happen because some parts of the atmosphere get more sunlight (and heat) than others. For example, air in the tropics gets more heat than air in the polar regions. Deserts heat up and cool down faster than oceans. These differences cause differences in air temperature. When air gets hot in one place, it expands and rises. Cold air from other places rushes in to fill the empty vacuum. That's the wind.

MAPPING THE WIND

Just as water flows over the land, the wind flows over the mountains, valleys, and other features of the earth. It follows patterns that we can predict, in the same way we can predict the currents in the ocean or where the Mississippi River flows in its banks.

A wind map can show us "lakes" of air where the wind is quiet, "streams" where it blows gently, and fast-moving wind "rivers."

The wind patterns in the entire world have already been mapped. These maps show us the best spots to put our wind power stations—places where the average wind is more than 15 miles per hour. Take a look at the wind map on the facing page and you can see that there is plenty of wind power in the United States.

Right now, wind power has the lowest cost of any form of renewable energy other than geothermal. It's almost cheap enough already to compete with fossil fuels. And new breakthroughs are sure to make wind power even cheaper in the near future.

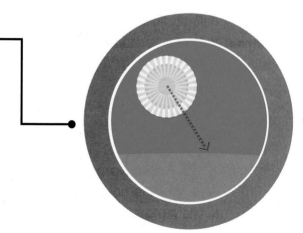

1. SUN HEATS AIR.

WIND RESOURCES IN THE U.S.

Just as solar power varies according to geography, the amount of energy we can harness from the wind depends on local conditions. The darkest green and blue areas show the best places for wind turbines.

WIND POWER DENSITY

On land
- FAIR
- GOOD
- EXCELLENT
- OUTSTANDING
- SUPERB

Offshore
- FAIR
- GOOD
- EXCELLENT
- OUTSTANDING
- SUPERB

● 10 LARGEST U.S. WIND FARMS PRODUCING MORE THAN 320 MW OF POWER ANNUALLY

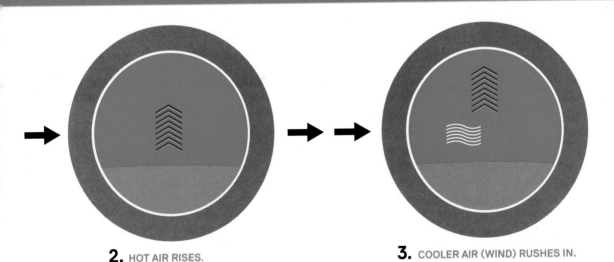

2. HOT AIR RISES.

3. COOLER AIR (WIND) RUSHES IN.

A MODERN WINDMILL

Modern windmills don't look much like the old-fashioned ones in Holland or the windmills used to pump water on ranches out west. Instead, they look like giant airplane propellers mounted on very tall towers. The blades of a turbine are shaped like aircraft wings. As the wind rushes over them, the shape creates "lift," helping the blades to turn.

Most turbines have three large blades 89 to 147 feet long. The towers are 147 to 344 feet tall. (The Statue of Liberty is 305 feet tall, including its base. The roadway of the Golden Gate Bridge is 220 feet above the water.)

When the wind is blowing, an average wind turbine can produce 1.5 megawatts of electricity. That's enough to supply all of the electricity needed by 400 American homes. Windmills are usually grouped in large "wind farms." Working together, 400 turbines can reach the output of a medium-size coal-burning power plant.

Early wind turbines made a lot of noise. Today, modern designs have made wind turbines much quieter, making it easier to put up wind farms near homes and towns.

A technician inspects a turbine blade at the Wethersfield wind farm in western New York.

HOW WIND BECOMES ELECTRICITY

Wind turbines are built in areas where there are regular, powerful winds. A group of turbines is called a wind farm. Wind farms can be built on land or out at sea.

The blades of a wind turbine are shaped like airplane wings. This shape makes the wind move differently on different sides of the blade. When wind hits the blades, it creates more pressure on one side than the other. That causes the blade to move, and the turbine spins.

Inside each wind turbine is an electricity generator. It works like the big generators at power plants. When the turbine blades spin, it turns the coil inside the generator and makes electricity.

THE UNITED STATES: A LEADER IN WIND

The United States produces more electricity from wind than any other country in the world. But that fact is misleading. Wind actually plays a very tiny part in supplying our energy needs. In 2007, less than 1 percent of the electricity in the U.S. came from wind power. Because we're such a big country, even 1 percent of our power is still a lot of electricity.

Other countries have done much better. Denmark is a small country that gets more than 21 percent of its electricity from windmills. One state in Germany gets 38.3 percent of its electricity from wind power. The Navarre region in northern Spain gets 70 percent of its electricity from windmills.

There are lots of places in the U.S. that have enough wind power to make electricity. We can easily add to our wind power if we choose. One advantage to wind turbines is that they can be built in a short time. It takes just two months to put one up. It takes several years to build a coal-fired power plant.

Other types of power plants, including concentrated solar, need a lot of water for making steam. Wind power does not use any water. In a world where water is becoming scarce, that is important. Wind turbines also take up less land than other types of power plants, although they are taller.

WIND ON THE WATER

Most windmills today are located on land. But there is a growing trend to put them offshore, sometimes miles from land. Winds at sea are usually steadier and more predictable. For decades, oil engineers have been building oil drilling platforms in deep water. Now we can use that same technology to build deep-water platforms for wind turbines.

Today, the world's largest offshore wind farm is in the ocean near Skegness, England. The wind farm has 54 huge windmills, each with blades more than 175 feet long. Together, these machines can produce enough electricity to power more than 130,000 homes.

HOME WINDMILLS

Just as people can put solar panels on their roofs, we can also install small windmills near our homes. These would have to be mostly in rural areas, where wind patterns are strong enough. Still,

Much of the United Kingdom's new wind power is based offshore, including this five-megawatt turbine near Inverness, Scotland.

THE BOY WHO HARNESSED THE WIND

It doesn't take a factory to build a wind turbine. Fourteen-year-old William Kamkwamba of Wimbe, Malawi, built one with the frame from his father's old bicycle, a rusted shock absorber, and a tractor fan. He used melted plastic pipes for the rotor blades and found some ball bearings in the town scrap heap. With a drill made of a corncob and a nail, and screwdrivers made from bicycle spokes, he built a windmill. When he was done, he put it on top of a ladder, the wind blew, the blades spun, and then William held a glowing electric bulb in his hand.

William was not in school at the time. His family could no longer afford the tuition. But William kept studying on his own. From an old physics textbook, he got the idea of building a wind turbine and bringing electricity to his town. He used diagrams of windmills he found in a library book.

Soon after his first success with the lightbulb, William got to work building a taller, more powerful windmill. He installed lightbulbs in every room of his family's house and two outside. Then William began installing solar panels to make even more electricity.

Today, thanks to William, every home in Wimbe has a solar panel and a battery to store power. A new windmill pumps water to irrigate his family's vegetable garden. A solar-powered pump at the public well fills water tanks for the whole town. And William is back in school, at the African Leadership Academy near Johannesburg, South Africa. And he's not done. He plans to start a company to build windmills in Africa.

You can read more about William on his blog, williamkamkwamba.typepad.com, and in his book, *The Boy Who Harnessed the Wind.*

William Kamkwamba high atop his homemade windmill.

there are about 13 million homes in the U.S. that could benefit from a small wind turbine.

Right now, the electricity from small turbines costs more than solar panels. However, that is likely to change as new turbine designs are invented. Even now, about 10,000 small windmills are being installed each year in the United States, and that number is rapidly increasing.

ARGUMENTS AGAINST WIND POWER

Some people worry about birds being killed when they fly into the blades of wind turbines. No one likes to see wildlife killed, but let's look at the facts. Thousands more birds are killed each year by flying into skyscrapers, by house cats, and by automobiles and pesticides than by windmills. On the other hand, stopping the climate crisis by cutting fossil fuel use will save whole species of birds from extinction. Still, engineers are working on ways to cut down on bird deaths from windmills. One solution is a sensor that will shut down the turbines when it detects a flock of birds.

Some people also think that windmills spoil views, but I believe windmills can be a beautiful addition to the landscape. They are especially beautiful if you imagine all the wildlife and habitats they are saving by allowing us to cut carbon pollution.

WIND-POWERED JOBS

Building, installing, and running thousands of new wind turbines means lots of new jobs for Americans. And these jobs can't be shipped overseas. Because towers, blades, and turbines are so big, it's much cheaper to build them in the country where they will be used. Already, tens of thousands of new jobs have been created in the United States in the wind power industry.

Of course, creating new jobs is just one reason to build wind turbines. The bigger reason is to help stop global warming.

Wind turbines are a proven and cheap way of getting clean, unlimited, renewable energy. As long as the sun keeps shining, the wind will keep blowing. That means we will have more than enough wind power to meet our needs and the needs of future generations. If we choose, we can harness the power of the wind, create a new carbon-free energy industry, and save our planet.

The Blue Lagoon spa in Iceland is fed by hot water from the geothermal power plant next door.

CHAPTER 5

THE POWER OF THE EARTH

Geothermal energy, from the heat of the earth, has enough power by itself to supply all of our energy needs.

Solar energy comes from the sun. Wind gets its power from the heat of sunlight. But there's another kind of renewable energy right under our feet. It's called *geothermal energy,* and it's the power of the earth.

Geothermal power comes from heat deep within the ground (*geo* = earth, *thermal* = heat). We see examples of this heat when volcanoes erupt. Natural hot springs or geysers, like Old Faithful in Yellowstone National Park, are also heated by geothermal energy.

The earth's crust is made up of giant continent-size pieces called *tectonic plates*. These plates float on the sea of molten magma in the earth's mantle. They actually move, although very, very slowly. Where these plates meet, at their edges, there are cracks that allow the magma to rise to the surface. That's why volcanoes (and earthquakes) are found around these cracks. If water is present in rocks heated by the magma, it may bubble up as a hot spring or geyser.

The very first hydrothermal power plant was built in 1904 at a site near Larderello, Italy. Today, there are hydrothermal plants working around the world. The largest hydrothermal plant on the planet is north of San Francisco at a hot spring called The Geysers. Twenty-two small power plants have been built in the area, and they have provided 60 percent of the electricity for California's North Coast.

Hydrothermal power plants work in different ways. Some use steam that comes directly from the ground. Some turn hot water from the ground into steam. A third method uses the hot underground water to boil some other liquid. In each case, the steam created turns a turbine to make electricity.

This kind of geothermal power is only available in places where there is a natural source of water underground. Also, the underground rocks must be *permeable*. That means water has to be able to flow through them.

The exciting news about geothermal power is that we are not limited to natural hydrothermal hot spots. Using the same drilling methods as the oil industry, we can basically create our own hot spots. This gives us a way to get almost unlimited geothermal power.

GEYSER

WATER HEATED BY HOT ROCKS

The 22 geothermal power plants of The Geysers in Northern California make up the largest geothermal installation in the world.

NEW GEOTHERMAL TECHNOLOGY

There is a new geothermal technology called *enhanced geothermal systems* (EGS). With EGS, we don't have to look for natural hydrothermal sites. Instead, geologists look for rocks underground that are at least 300°F. Then they drill down, as far as two miles or even farther. They pump high-pressure water into these rocks. This splits the rocks and creates a path for water to flow.

Once the system is in place, engineers can pump water through the hot rocks. The water becomes superheated (or sometimes is turned into steam). A second set of pipes is used to bring that hot water up to the surface. There it's used to power a turbine and make electricity.

One problem with EGS is that drilling deep into the earth can sometimes trigger an earthquake. Although such a quake would be very small, engineers still have to take steps to avoid one. This means carefully choosing where to drill. Sensors

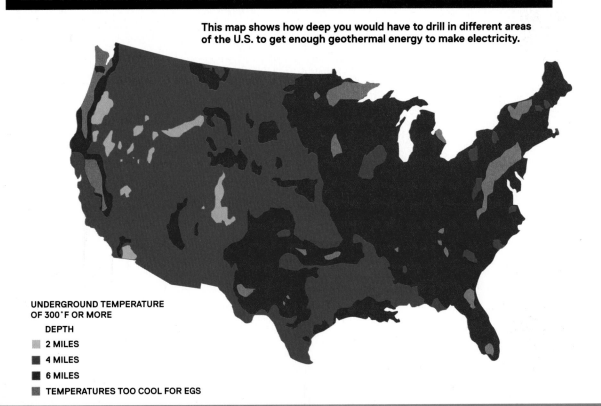

GEOTHERMAL ENERGY SOURCES IN THE UNITED STATES

This map shows how deep you would have to drill in different areas of the U.S. to get enough geothermal energy to make electricity.

UNDERGROUND TEMPERATURE OF 300°F OR MORE

DEPTH

■ 2 MILES

■ 4 MILES

■ 6 MILES

■ TEMPERATURES TOO COOL FOR EGS

HOW GEOTHERMAL POWER SYSTEMS WORK

In the newest form of geothermal power systems, holes are drilled two to four miles into the earth to [...] that are at least 300°F. The rock is broken up so water can flow through it. Then water is pumped do[...] through the rocks. It comes back up as heated water. That heat is used to make steam and generate [...]

POWER TRANSMISSION

POWER PL[...]

TURBINE

GENERA[...]

HEAT EXCHANGER

INJECTION PUMP

SEDIMENTARY LAYER

COOL WATER

HOT WATER

HOT ROCK

ROCK IS CRUSHED
SO WATER CAN FLOW
THROUGH

MY OWN GEOTHERMAL ENERGY

There's another way to get energy out of the ground—with your own geothermal heat pump. These heat pumps are small enough for many homeowners to use. Instead of needing to go down a mile or more underground, these home energy pumps usually only need to go down a few hundred feet or so. That's about as deep as many water wells. In 2007, my wife and I decided to have one of these heat pump systems installed in our own home. Here's how it works: A local company drilled a few holes in my driveway. The holes go down about 300 feet. At that depth, the temperature of the soil is always 59°F.

Why does the soil down there stay at the same temperature? All of the ground above it acts as a big layer of insulation. So the soil at that depth stays at the year-round average air temperature in our part of Tennessee.

Our heat pump is very simple. It's called a *direct exchange* system, or DX. A type of liquid called a *refrigerant* is sent down into the ground in pipes. (This is the same kind of liquid used in air conditioners.) When the cool liquid goes through the underground pipes, it is heated to 59 degrees. That heat energy is brought back up and used to heat our house.

Of course, most people want their houses warmer than 59 degrees in the winter. So we have to add a little extra heat to our system to get the temperature up a few more degrees. But it takes a lot less energy to heat the air from 59 degrees to 68 than if we started with cold winter air at 32 degrees or less. As a result, we need much less energy from other sources.

In the summer, the opposite happens. Warm liquid is sent down and it is cooled to 59 degrees. That keeps our house nice and cool. And the system is silent, so we don't have to listen to the hum of the air conditioner.

SUMMER COOLING MODE

WINTER HEATING MODE

can also warn if a drill is going to start a quake so it can be shut down in time.

Geothermal technology has made great advances in recent years. Scientists tell us it is ready to be a major source of energy. Right now, most EGS wells are two to four miles deep. Heat at this depth can be used to make electricity.

It can also be used directly to heat buildings. In Boise, Idaho, the state capitol and many other buildings have long been heated with geothermal water. In Klamath Falls, Oregon, homes have been using geothermal wells for more than a century. In Iceland, almost every building in the country is heated by geothermal water.

But in some places, the heat four miles down is not enough. If drill technology can be improved, we can sink EGS wells down to six miles. When that happens, geothermal power will be available in many more areas.

The amount of money needed for geothermal research is tiny compared to most government research budgets. Yet geothermal power has not received the funding it needs. Many people still have the idea that geothermal power is not as important a resource as solar or wind power. This is a big mistake.

We should be developing geothermal power at top speed.

It's important to understand that geothermal power is ready to be used today. While the United States was asleep, other nations began to research and develop EGS. The Philippines, El Salvador, and Costa Rica have all recently achieved the production of more than 15 percent of their electricity from geothermal generation. So have Kenya and Iceland.

New Zealand, Indonesia, Nicaragua, and the Caribbean island of Guadeloupe all get between 5 and 10 percent of their electricity from geothermal generation. The European Union has an EGS project under way in Soultz-sous-Forêts, France. Other projects are being built right now in Germany, Switzerland, the United Kingdom, the Czech Republic, and elsewhere.

These projects show that there's a third renewable resource for fighting the climate crisis. Like solar and wind power, it can supply all of our energy needs. All we have to do is harness it. The power is literally right under our feet.

Sugarcane being harvested in Sertãozinho, Brazil. Brazil has developed the first large-scale biofuel economy by making ethanol from sugarcane. About 50 percent of fuel used in gas-powered cars there is ethanol.

CAN WE GROW OUR FUEL?

We can get energy by burning plants—and reduce the global warming pollution we put into the air.

Throughout history, people have used plants for energy. Today, millions of people still burn wood to heat their homes and cook their food. They also burn peat, which is soil that contains a lot of plant matter. Even animal manure can be burned for energy because it contains the remains of plants. All of these sources of energy are called *biomass*.

When wood is burned in a fireplace or trees are burned in a forest, carbon dioxide, black carbon, and other global warming pollution goes into the air. But modern technology has given us new ways to turn plants into energy without adding as much global warming pollution to the air.

Advanced furnaces can burn biomass at high temperatures, which makes energy more efficiently. The heat can be used to make steam to power turbines or to heat houses. Crops or even weeds can be turned into ethanol fuel and used to power cars. Landfills—the huge garbage dumps of cities—can be tapped for methane gas, which can then be burned for electricity.

Biomass is a renewable energy source because plants get their energy from the sun. As long as the sun keeps shining, we can grow new plants for energy.

With the right technology, biomass can be a good replacement for fossil fuels—and a good solution for the climate crisis.

ETHANOL: FUEL FROM PLANTS

Burning biomass does release carbon dioxide, just as burning fossil fuels like gasoline or coal does. However, there is one important difference. When we burn a fossil fuel, we release carbon that's been sitting in the ground for hundreds of millions of years. When we do that, we are changing the balance of carbon between the earth and the atmosphere. It's like adding "new" carbon to the carbon cycle.

Biomass, unlike fossil fuels, is a part of the carbon cycle. The carbon in biomass came from the air, not the ground. When we burn plants, we return the carbon to the air, but then next year's crop will take it back out again. As long as we plant new crops that soak up the carbon, we can keep the carbon cycle in balance.

The best-known type of *biofuel* (made from biomass) is ethanol. Ethanol is a kind of alcohol that is made from plants. Basically, ethanol is made with yeast, a kind of fungus. The yeast feeds on the sugars (carbohydrates) in plants. It turns the carbohydrates into alcohol. Then the alcohol (ethanol) can be burned in cars and trucks instead of gasoline. Most cars can burn up to 10 percent ethanol mixed with gasoline.

Burning ethanol in cars is not a new idea. As far back as 1908, Henry Ford designed his Model T to run on a mixture of gasoline and ethanol. However, it is only recently that the idea has become popular again. Many people hope that ethanol can be a good

THE CARBON CYCLE

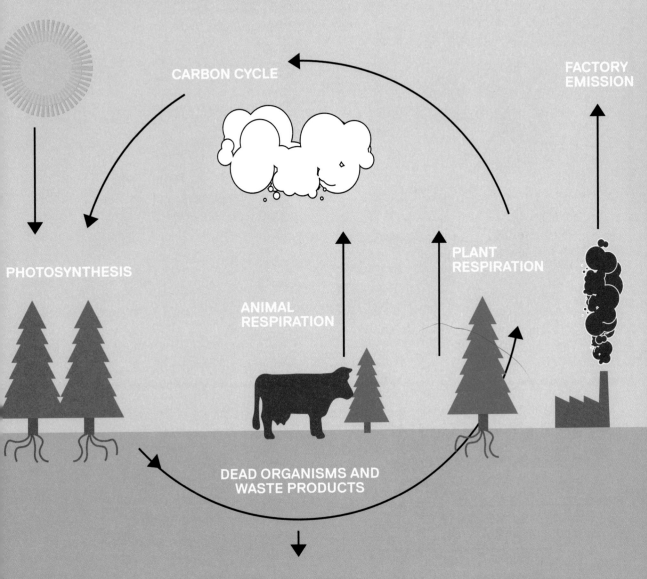

CARBON CYCLE

FACTORY EMISSION

PHOTOSYNTHESIS

ANIMAL RESPIRATION

PLANT RESPIRATION

DEAD ORGANISMS AND WASTE PRODUCTS

1. In photosynthesis, plants store energy from sunlight by making carbohydrates. They make the carbohydrates from carbon dioxide in the air, nutrients in the soil, and water. Plants breathe out oxygen.

2. Animals eat plants and use the carbohydrates for energy. Animals breathe in oxygen and breathe out carbon dioxide, returning it to the air.

3. When plants and animals die, their bodies decay. Some of the carbon in their bodies becomes part of the soil. Some is released into the air.

4. When fossil fuels are burned, carbon dioxide is released.

HOW ETHANOL IS MADE

Ethanol is made from carbohydrates—sugars—that are made by plants. There are two ways to get sugar from plants. The first way uses crops like corn and sugarcane. The plants are ground up and "cooked" with enzymes, chemicals that break the carbohydrates into sugar. The second way is to use plants like switchgrass. To get at the sugar in these plants, the woody cell walls (made of cellulose) have to be broken down. Once you have sugar, you can use yeast to turn the sugar into ethanol.

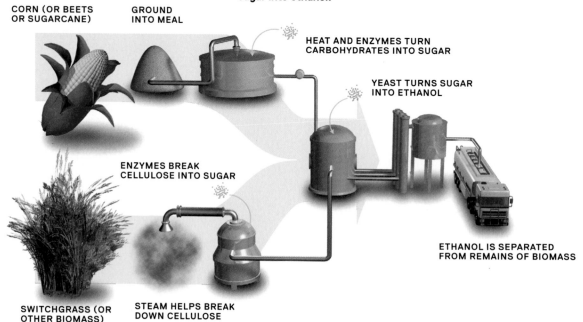

CORN (OR BEETS OR SUGARCANE)

GROUND INTO MEAL

HEAT AND ENZYMES TURN CARBOHYDRATES INTO SUGAR

YEAST TURNS SUGAR INTO ETHANOL

ENZYMES BREAK CELLULOSE INTO SUGAR

ETHANOL IS SEPARATED FROM REMAINS OF BIOMASS

SWITCHGRASS (OR OTHER BIOMASS)

STEAM HELPS BREAK DOWN CELLULOSE

solution to global warming and cut our need to import foreign oil.

CORN OR CANE?

Right now, most of the ethanol we make in the United States comes from corn. This is very popular with farmers and with big agriculture companies. It is also popular with politicians who represent farming districts. I should know. When I was a young congressman from a farming district in Tennessee, I was strongly in favor of ethanol. (Back then it was called *gasohol*.)

But it turns out that corn is not the best material for making ethanol. It takes a lot of energy to make ethanol, and most of the energy comes from fossil fuels. Also, the way most farmers grow corn uses a lot of fossil fuels—to power tractors and other machines and to make fertilizer. That means more carbon dioxide and

Corn is grown to make ethanol near the Cottam Power Station in Nottinghamshire, England.

Trucks filled with sugarcane line up at an ethanol plant near São Paulo, Brazil.

global warming pollution. If you add it all up, making corn-based ethanol produces almost the same amount of greenhouse gas as the gasoline it replaces. That's why I now believe making ethanol from corn this way is a mistake.

In Brazil, they make ethanol from sugarcane, with much better results. First, it takes a lot less fossil fuel to grow sugarcane than corn, especially in the tropics. Second, sugarcane contains a lot more energy than corn. One acre of corn can produce 400 gallons of ethanol. One acre of sugarcane produces 650 gallons of the biofuel. And making ethanol from sugarcane releases only one third the greenhouse gas emissions as making ethanol from corn.

There's another problem with corn-based ethanol. When power companies compete with food companies for corn, the price of corn goes up. Because we use

TURNING CROPS INTO FUEL

Some crops are a better source of fuel than others. This graph shows how many gallons of fuel can be produced from one acre of crops.

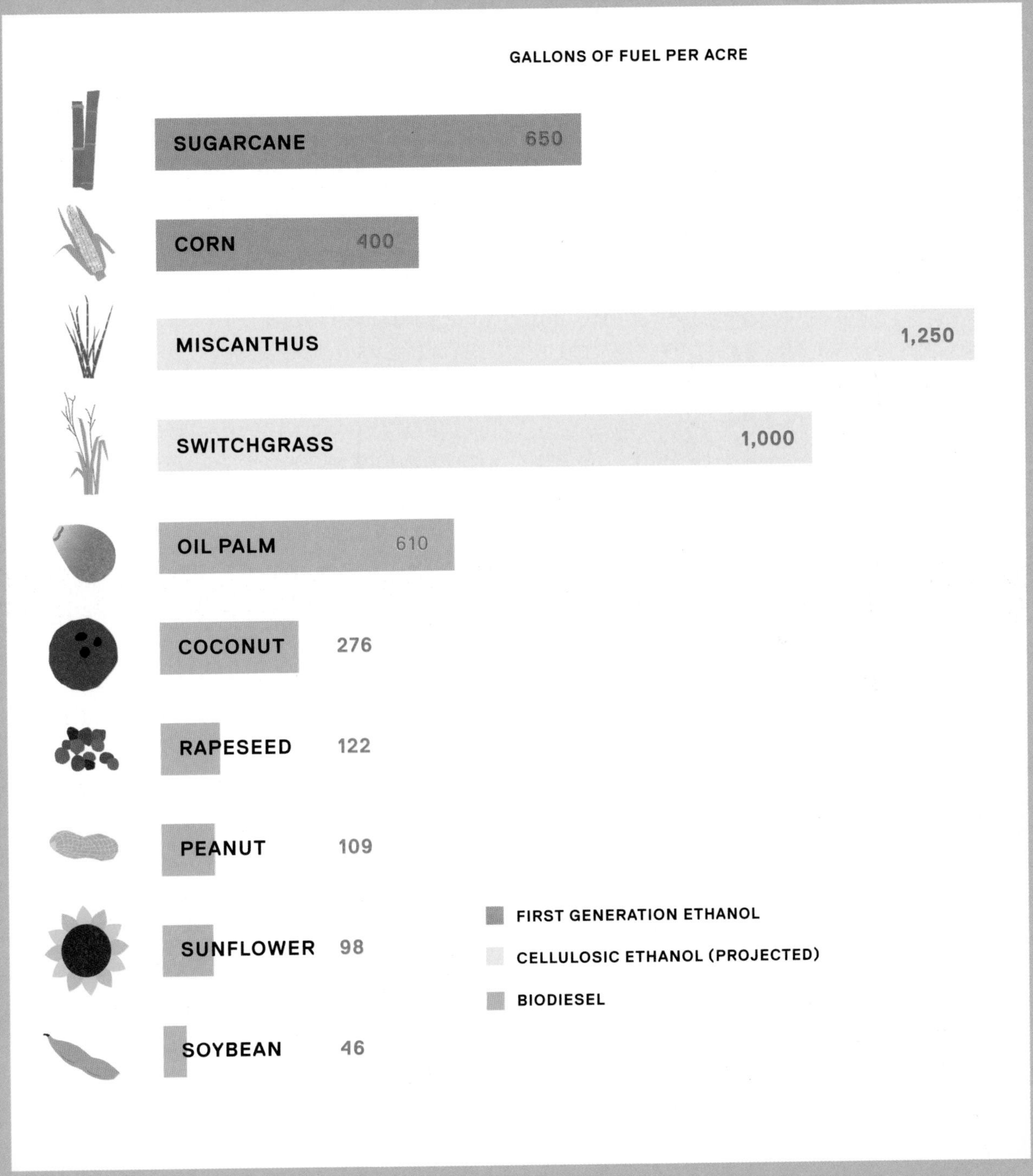

GALLONS OF FUEL PER ACRE

Crop	Gallons
SUGARCANE	650
CORN	400
MISCANTHUS	1,250
SWITCHGRASS	1,000
OIL PALM	610
COCONUT	276
RAPESEED	122
PEANUT	109
SUNFLOWER	98
SOYBEAN	46

- FIRST GENERATION ETHANOL
- CELLULOSIC ETHANOL (PROJECTED)
- BIODIESEL

corn to make so many other foods, when the price of corn goes up, the price of all foods goes up. If we increase ethanol production, it might add to the danger of worldwide food shortages. And even if we used all the corn produced in the U.S. to make ethanol, it would still only supply about 13 percent of our fuel needs.

Finally, making corn-based ethanol uses large amounts of water. It takes four gallons of water to make one gallon of ethanol. That's on top of the average 142 gallons needed just to grow the corn.

Miscanthus, also called elephant grass, is a promising biofuel crop. It is low maintenance, easy to cultivate, and grows very quickly.

Water is a limited and shrinking resource in the world today. We must find ways to get our energy that do not require more water.

FUEL FROM GRASS

Today, energy companies are working on new ways to make ethanol—ways that produce more energy while releasing less greenhouse gas. One is to use more of the plant—not just the carbohydrates. Most of a plant is made of *cellulose*. That's the woody material that gives plants their structure. Cellulosic ethanol is made by breaking down cellulose and turning it into ethanol.

Cellulosic ethanol can be made from just about any plant, including grasses. Switchgrass is one example. In most places, people think of switchgrass as a weed. Yet it's a very good source for ethanol. It can be grown on land that is not suitable for food crops and it does not need artificial (fossil fuel) fertilizer. And grasses grow back after they are cut, so they do not need to be planted every year like corn. On top of every-thing else, switchgrass takes carbon out of the air and stores it in the soil.

Fast-growing trees can also be used for cellulosic ethanol. So can wood waste from the timber industry like scraps and brush. However, cellulosic ethanol is still in the early stages of development. There are at least two different methods being tested. It will take a while before we know if it will really be a good substitute for gasoline.

PLANT POWER

Because of ethanol, most Americans think of biofuel as something you put in a gas tank. But many scientists think the best use of biomass is to burn it directly, without first turning it into liquid fuel like ethanol.

Every step of turning corn into car fuel loses energy. By the time you burn it in a car engine, you have lost as much as 90 percent of the original energy in the plant. On the other hand, if you turn biomass directly into heat, you can use about 60 percent of the energy stored in the plant.

In Europe, two thirds of renewable energy comes from the direct burning of biomass. Wood, wood scraps, and other biomass fuels are burned in modern furnaces. The furnaces are designed to collect toxic waste from the smoke. They also waste far less energy than coal-fired power plants.

FRENCH FRY POWER

Ethanol is not the only biofuel you can put in a gas tank. Cars and trucks with diesel engines can run on vegetable oil. Cars can even run on used fry grease from restaurants (although the car exhaust smells like french fries). Other cars run on a mixture of vegetable oil and diesel fuel, called *biodiesel*. Biodiesel creates less pollution than regular diesel. However, because biodiesel is made from food crops like corn and soybeans, it is not a good solution to the climate crisis.

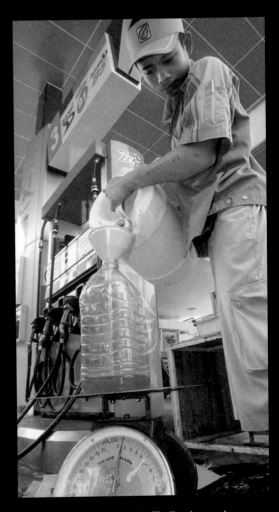

At a gas station in Bangkok, Thailand, a worker fills a container with used vegetable oil that will be processed to make biodiesel.

Many companies in the U.S. timber industry also use biomass generators. They have a steady supply of wood scraps and use the heat for their buildings or to generate electricity. In addition, some coal-fired power plants also burn biomass. Wood and other biomass fuels can replace up to 20 percent of the coal a power plant uses.

One advantage of biomass generators is that they can run 24 hours a day and supply electricity when solar or wind power is not available. Burning biomass to generate heat and electricity should be an important part of our renewable energy system.

GARBAGE POWER

There's another important source of biomass. It's cheap and there is plenty of it. It's trapped inside huge landfills all over the world. These giant garbage dumps are full of food waste like rotting plants and vegetables. As the plants decay, they give off methane—which is basically the same as natural gas.

When methane escapes from a landfill, it goes into the atmosphere and adds to the greenhouse effect. But if you can trap the methane, you can burn it to heat houses or use in cooking stoves. You can also burn it to make electricity. Some cities have cars and trucks that run on landfill gas. So methane is valuable. Businesses could make money from our garbage heaps by mining methane.

The technology for capturing methane from landfills is already in use. In the most common method, a series of vertical wells are drilled into the landfill. The gas seeps into the wells and then it is piped to a collection point.

In 1996, the Environmental Protection Agency set up a new "Landfill Rule." This requires all new landfills to capture the methane they produce. However, many cities that do collect landfill gas just burn

Some landfills now capture a portion of the methane escaping from their decaying organic matter. The gas from this landfill in New Jersey helps power 25,000 local homes.

This small German village generates all of its heating and electricity from biomass, including wood chips and animal waste.

it. That at least turns the methane into carbon dioxide, which is not as powerful a greenhouse gas. It would be much better for the environment if the methane were used as an energy source.

Many companies have teamed up with landfill operators to generate electricity and heat from landfill gas. For example, the BMW auto plant in Greer, South Carolina, gets 70 percent of its energy needs from landfill gas. The company estimates that in six years it has saved $5 million in energy costs every year by using landfill gas.

SMART BIOFUELS

Biofuels can be an important source of renewable energy, but only if they are produced and used in the right way. For example, forests in Indonesia have been cut down to plant oil palm trees. That was because there was a tax break in the U.S. for using palm oil to make biodiesel. Cutting down forests to make biofuel is clearly not a good thing. It adds to the climate crisis and destroys animal habitats.

Governments around the world are beginning to set rules for producing and using biofuel. These rules all have one aim: to make sure that biofuels don't add to the climate crisis, but help end it. That means growing biofuels without chopping down forests and without taking the place of food crops. It means producing biofuels without creating extra CO_2 and without using large amounts of water.

So, yes, we can grow our fuel. And if we're smart about how we do it, biomass can help us grow our way out of global warming.

The In Salah CCS Project in Algeria puts about one million tons of CO$_2$ underground each year.

CHAPTER 7

CAN WE CAPTURE CARBO$_2$N?

Can we capture the carbon dioxide from burning coal before it goes into the atmosphere?

Here's a great idea: what if we could burn all the coal we want without adding CO_2 to the air? In other words, what if we could burn coal without adding to global warming? This simple idea has a big name: *carbon capture and sequestration* (CCS). It's an idea that has been around for some time.

Very simply, CCS means collecting all of the CO_2 released from burning coal (that's the capture part) and burying it somewhere in the earth (sequestration). If it worked, coal would stop being a giant source of greenhouse gas. If it worked, we could keep burning coal for electricity without destroying the world's climate.

If it worked. And that's the problem with CCS.

The reality is that after decades of trying, no one has built a large-scale coal-fired power plant where CCS works the way it has to before we can use it to stop global warming.

To make CCS work, you have to do three things:
1. You have to capture the CO_2 before it goes up a smokestack.
2. You have to turn the gas into a liquid (or liquidlike) form so you can transport it.
3. You have to find places where you can safely bury it in the ground.

Making all three things happen has turned out to be very difficult and expensive.

Liquid CO_2 is already being used as a way to get oil out of the ground. The CO_2 is pumped into the ground, where it pushes oil toward the surface.

One big problem with CCS technology is that it eats up a huge amount of energy. For a coal-fired power plant to capture all of its carbon dioxide, it would need to use between 25 and 35 percent more energy. That means a plant would have to burn one-third more coal just to produce the same amount of power for consumers. Or it would have to produce one-third less electricity from the same amount of coal.

The coal industry argues that burning extra coal would be okay, because in the end, no CO_2 would be released into the air. But if you look more closely, you see that there are several problems with this plan. First, burning more coal would cost a lot of money. That means the price of electricity from coal would climb. Second, all of the carbon dioxide released while mining and transporting the extra coal would not be captured.

And let's not forget all the other environmental problems caused by coal mining. Coal mining these days often means chopping the tops off of mountains and dumping tons of toxic waste into streams and valleys. The waste includes arsenic, lead, cadmium, and other dangerous forms of pollution, which often seep into drinking-water supplies.

Coal companies now cut the tops off mountains, like this one, and dump the waste into rivers and valleys. Burning more coal will cause more environmental damage like this.

Carbon dioxide is not the only form of pollution that comes out of coal power plants, either. There are sulfur oxides, which cause acid rain. And then there's nitrogen oxide, which causes smog. Power plants also dump tons of mercury into the air every year. Mercury is a powerful poison that can cause nerve and brain damage.

On top of all that, coal plants create pollution even after the coal is burnt.

▶▶ **U.S. coal plants produce 130 million tons of coal ash and sludge each year. This is one of the largest streams of industrial waste in the country.**

Getting rid of it all is already a big problem. Tons of coal ash are dumped into old mines where the poisons can seep into groundwater. The rest is put into giant pits called coal ash ponds. In my home state of Tennessee, three days before Christmas 2008, one of these ponds broke, and one billion gallons of this toxic sludge burst out and destroyed a neighborhood in the town of Harriman.

WHERE DO YOU PUT IT?

Capturing carbon dioxide before it goes into the air is a difficult job. It would be even harder in many of the older coal plants in the nation. But it could be done—at great expense. The problem we would then face is what to do with all of the CO_2 we capture.

The most likely way to store CO_2 is as a liquid, deep underground. And there would be a lot of liquid CO_2 to store. The CO_2 from all U.S. coal-burning power plants would fill 30 million barrels a day. We'd have to build a nationwide network of pipelines to move it from the power plants to the storage areas.

The liquid CO_2 has to be put deep into the earth where it won't escape. It has to be put where there is no chance of an earthquake that would create leaks that could reach the surface. Each site is different, and each has to be studied carefully. So far, only relatively small storage areas have been tried out.

What would happen if the CO_2 managed to make its way up to the surface? First of all, it would enter the atmosphere and add to global warming. That would defeat the entire purpose of CCS.

HOW CARBON CAPTURE WORKS

Carbon capture and sequestration is based on the idea that carbon from power plants can be stored underground. Carbon dioxide is captured in the smokestacks of a power plant. It is then turned into a liquid and pumped underground. It could be stored in oil and natural gas deposits that have been partly emptied by wells. That would help force the remaining oil or gas up out of the ground. Or the liquid carbon could be stored in natural rock formations.

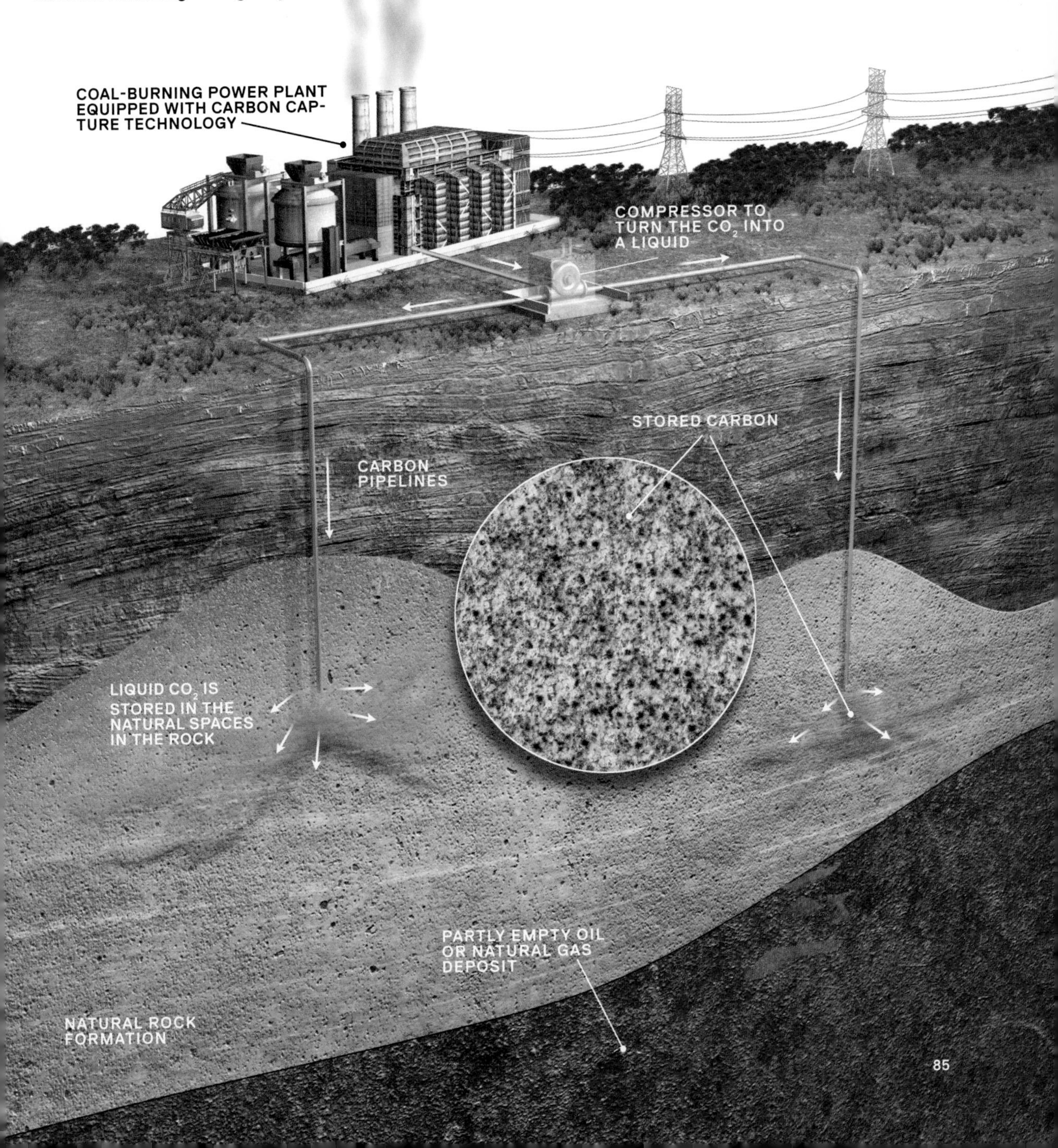

COAL-BURNING POWER PLANT EQUIPPED WITH CARBON CAPTURE TECHNOLOGY

COMPRESSOR TO TURN THE CO_2 INTO A LIQUID

STORED CARBON

CARBON PIPELINES

LIQUID CO_2 IS STORED IN THE NATURAL SPACES IN THE ROCK

PARTLY EMPTY OIL OR NATURAL GAS DEPOSIT

NATURAL ROCK FORMATION

We have to handle it carefully for another reason. In 1986, a large amount of naturally produced carbon dioxide bubbled up from the bottom of a lake in the African nation of Cameroon. When the gas burst out of the lake, it settled near the ground and cut off oxygen to the local residents. More than 1,700 people died as a result.

Most experts agree that such a tragedy could not happen from carbon dioxide stored underground. Scientists have a good idea of where safe storage of CO_2 is possible. But this story shows why we can't afford to take any shortcuts in studying and choosing storage sites.

DO WE NEED CCS?

In spite of the problems with CCS, some people feel we have no choice but to try to make it work. After all, the climate crisis is so serious we can't afford to throw out any possible solution. Even though CCS is expensive, the effects of global warming are a lot worse. And there's another point in favor of CCS. If it worked, we wouldn't have to shut down all of our coal power plants.

At present, there are several projects that are testing places for burying CO_2.

The Sleipner Gas Field in the North Sea near Norway is the first commercial CCS project in the world.

HOW MUCH COAL IS THERE?

The U.S. government is spending billions of taxpayer dollars to develop CCS technology. Part of the argument for spending all that money is that the U.S. has a 250-year supply of coal. That number is often quoted, yet there is no proof that this is so.

The National Research Council, an organization whose job is to advise Congress on matters of science, says the United States probably has more than a 100-year supply of coal, but that number goes down if we start using coal at a higher rate.

That's still a lot of coal, but it shows that coal, unlike sun or wind power, is a limited resource.

Large piles of coal in Tanggu Port, Tianjin, China

Most of these are deep in working oil fields. As the CO_2 is pumped in, it helps force the remaining oil out of the ground. An oil field in Saskatchewan, Canada, is an international test site for this method. There's also a test project in the North Sea oil fields off Norway and several others around the world. However, none of these projects handles the huge amounts of CO_2 that full-scale CCS would capture.

The largest CCS project in the U.S. is called FutureGen. FutureGen plans to build a full-scale CCS power plant in Mattoon, Illinois. The company says it will be able to generate 90 percent carbon-free electricity from coal. However, the project has been on the drawing board since 2003 and was even canceled in 2008. In 2009, Congress voted to restart it.

There's also a proposal for a CCS plant in Linden, New Jersey, near New York City. The idea is that the plant would make electricity during the peak demand hours of the day and make fertilizer at night. All the CO_2 from the plant would be piped 70 miles offshore and buried beneath the bottom of the Atlantic Ocean.

THE COST OF CARBON

Some of these projects might turn out to be successful. But none of them proves that CCS is ready—now—as a solution to the climate crisis.

In spite of this, the coal industry has worked hard to convince the public that CCS is ready today. They say they should be allowed to build new coal-burning power plants, because later these will be fitted with CCS technology.

The coal industry has not invested the huge sums needed to make CCS a reality. And they won't—until we charge polluters for releasing CO_2 into the air. If releasing carbon dioxide has a high price, then the coal industry will work very hard to figure out ways to make CCS work.

If they do, then someday CCS might be part of a carbon-free energy system, alongside wind and solar power. But that day is not today.

The Three Mile Island nuclear power plant in Pennsylvania suffered a partial meltdown in 1979. Only one of the two reactors is still active.

CHAPTER 8

SHOULD WE GO NUCLEAR?

Nuclear power plants make electricity without creating any global warming pollution. But nuclear power will probably not be a very big part of the solution to the climate crisis.

Nuclear power, the power of the atom, has two sides. One is the terrible, frightening power of the atom bomb. The other side is the promise of inexpensive electricity that does not greatly add to global warming.

Fifty years ago, scientists told us that nuclear power would solve all of our energy needs. Then, in the 1970s, people became very worried about the safety of nuclear power plants. Since then, the U.S. nuclear power industry has been at a standstill. No nuclear plants ordered in this country after 1972 have been completed.

But global warming has made people take a closer look at nuclear power. Nuclear plants can produce electricity without creating large amounts of greenhouse gases. Could they be a big part of the solution to the climate crisis? I believe the answer is probably no.

SPLITTING THE ATOM

Do you know Einstein's famous formula, $E=MC^2$? One thing it says, to put it very simply, is that a tiny amount of matter can give off a tremendous amount of energy. If that energy is released all at once, you get an atomic explosion. If you release it in a controlled way, in a nuclear reactor, you can get a lot of heat from a small amount of fuel.

In a nuclear reactor, one pound of uranium can give off as much energy as three million pounds of coal.

The power in a nuclear reactor comes from splitting the core of an atom, the nucleus. This splitting is called *fission.* As you probably know, the nuclei of atoms are made up of neutrons and protons. When the bonds that hold the protons and neutrons together are broken, large amounts of energy are released.

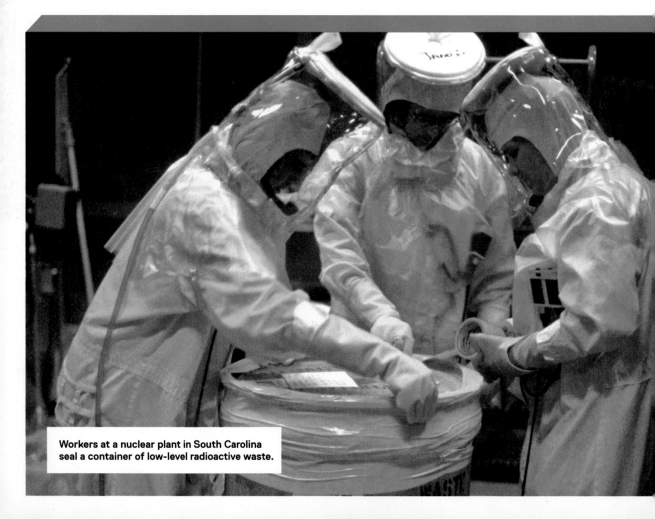

Workers at a nuclear plant in South Carolina seal a container of low-level radioactive waste.

HOW A NUCLEAR POWER PLANT WORKS

Radioactive material (usually uranium) is made into fuel rods. The rods are kept in a containment structure to seal off the deadly radiation. When the rods are near one another, a controlled chain reaction begins. That releases a lot of energy as heat. A liquid is pumped through the containment structure and turned into steam. Then it is used to power a turbine.

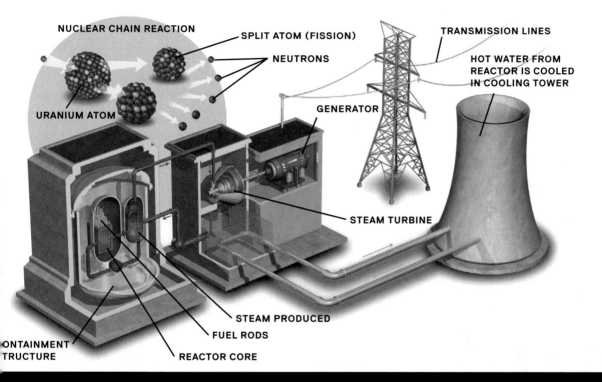

NUCLEAR CHAIN REACTION

SPLIT ATOM (FISSION)

NEUTRONS

URANIUM ATOM

TRANSMISSION LINES

HOT WATER FROM REACTOR IS COOLED IN COOLING TOWER

GENERATOR

STEAM TURBINE

STEAM PRODUCED

FUEL RODS

CONTAINMENT STRUCTURE

REACTOR CORE

Uranium is the fuel used in most nuclear reactors. When the nucleus of a uranium atom is hit by a free neutron, it splits. This releases large amounts of heat and radiation. Radiation is a kind of energy and can take many forms. The radiation from a nuclear reaction can be deadly.

When the nucleus of a uranium atom splits, it releases more free neutrons. If one of those neutrons hits another uranium atom, that nucleus will split too, releasing more energy and neutrons. This is called a *chain reaction*.

If there is enough uranium present, a chain reaction can become a nuclear explosion. But nuclear power reactors are designed to prevent explosions. The chain reaction is controlled with rods of material that absorb some of the flying neutrons. These control rods fit in between the nuclear material and slow down or stop the chain reaction.

BUT IS IT SAFE?

Once a chain reaction has started, the way a nuclear reactor works is basically the same as a coal or even a concentrated solar plant. The heat from the chain reaction is used to boil water and make steam. The pressure of the steam turns a turbine, which turns a generator, which makes electricity.

No carbon dioxide or other greenhouse gases are released while operating a nuclear power plant. Some countries, like France, get most of their electricity from nuclear power. So why don't we?

Nuclear power stalled in this country because many people had questions about its safety. First, there are fears about possible accidents. At Three Mile Island, in Pennsylvania, in March 1979, a nuclear power plant came close to a meltdown. That means that the chain reaction was out of control. In a meltdown, there is a risk that the thick walls of the reactor could be broken and large amounts of deadly radiation could escape.

Tragically, that is what happened in 1986 at a reactor at Chernobyl, near the border between Ukraine and Belarus. The chain reaction got out of control, the containment walls were destroyed, and a huge cloud of radiation was released. More than 4,000 people will ultimately lose their lives because of the accident. Some 350,000 had to leave their homes.

Radiation from reactor explosions can settle thousands of miles away. Some

I visited Chernobyl in 1988 and saw the reactor whose core had melted down. I walked through the ghost town that was left of the city. The accident released more than 100 times as much radiation as the atomic bombs dropped on Nagasaki and Hiroshima in Japan at the end of World War II.

NUCLEAR POWER AROUND THE WORLD

Right now there are more than 436 active nuclear reactors around the world. The United States has 104 active reactors, which make almost 31 percent of all nuclear-generated electricity in the world.

SWEDEN
10

FINLAND
4

LITHUANIA
1

NETHERLANDS
1

GERMANY
17

SLOVAKIA
4

RUSSIA
31

CANADA
18

U.K.
19

UKRAINE
15

BELGIUM
7

FRANCE
59

ARMENIA
1

JAPAN
53

U.S.
104

SPAIN
8

ROMANIA
2

CHINA
(AND TAIWAN)
17

SWITZERLAND
5

MEXICO
2

CZECH REPUBLIC
6

BULGARIA
2

INDIA
17

SOUTH KOREA
20

SLOVENIA
1

PAKISTAN
2

HUNGARY
4

BRAZIL
2

SOUTH AFRICA
2

ARGENTINA
2

☐ HAS NUCLEAR-POWERED ENERGY
(with number of reactors)

☐ HAS NUCLEAR-POWERED ENERGY
AND NUCLEAR WEAPONS
(with number of reactors)

radiation from Chernobyl fell on Wales, in the United Kingdom. The toxic material can stay in the ground for a very long time, causing the risk of serious illnesses.

There are other safety problems with nuclear power plants. One is nuclear waste. Once the uranium in the reactor has been used up, it still gives off deadly radiation and will do so for many thousands of years. After decades, the U.S. still has not decided where to permanently store our deadly nuclear waste. A plan to bury it deep under the desert in Nevada has been canceled.

NUCLEAR ROADBLOCKS

These safety questions are very real, but I believe that in time, they can

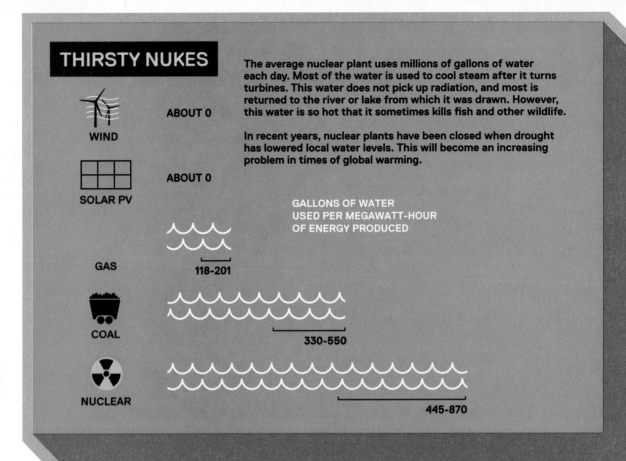

THIRSTY NUKES

WIND — ABOUT 0

SOLAR PV — ABOUT 0

The average nuclear plant uses millions of gallons of water each day. Most of the water is used to cool steam after it turns turbines. This water does not pick up radiation, and most is returned to the river or lake from which it was drawn. However, this water is so hot that it sometimes kills fish and other wildlife.

In recent years, nuclear plants have been closed when drought has lowered local water levels. This will become an increasing problem in times of global warming.

GALLONS OF WATER
USED PER MEGAWATT-HOUR
OF ENERGY PRODUCED

GAS — 118-201

COAL — 330-550

NUCLEAR — 445-870

probably be solved. The problem is, we do not have time to wait. We have to find new ways of making electricity now. Nuclear power plants probably can't play a much bigger role than they do now because they cost too much and take much too long to build.

It turns out that electricity from nuclear power is very expensive. The estimated cost of building a nuclear power plant rose from around $400 million in the 1970s to $4 billion in the 1990s. And that

is just an estimated cost. No one can predict how much a new nuclear plant will really cost. It takes 15 to 20 years to build a plant, and the price can go up as much as $1 billion for each year of construction.

Some people say that government is the problem, that there are too many regulations that slow down the building of nuclear plants. But these regulations have already been made simpler, and some are needed to keep the plants safe. The real problem is that nuclear plants are very complicated to build. Nuclear power plants cannot be mass-produced like PV solar panels. Most have been built from scratch, with a new set of plans. In fact, most of the 436 nuclear power plants in the world are based on different designs. There is a shortage of engineers who know how to build and run them. There is also a shortage of parts. For example, only one company, in Japan, builds a key part for all the reactors in the world. And they only build four a year.

ELECTRICITY OR BOMBS?

There's another problem with building lots of new nuclear reactors—a big problem. With the right technology, the fuel used in reactors can be made into a key component of atomic bombs. When I was Vice President, I saw firsthand how "peaceful" nuclear plants could be used as part of a nuclear weapons program.

Building a nuclear plant enables a country to train nuclear scientists and engineers. Those same scientists and engineers can be forced by a dictator to work secretly on a nuclear weapons program. Indeed, that is the main way nuclear weapons have spread in the past 25 years.

If we decide to solve the climate crisis with nuclear power, how can we keep nuclear weapons from spreading at the same time?

NUKES ARE NOT THE ANSWER

Scientists are currently working on at least 100 new designs for nuclear power plants. Some use a different kind of nuclear reaction called *fusion*. Some use a different type of fuel that is much safer and can't be made into weapons. However, all of these technologies will take a long time to develop. It might be as long as 25 years before the next generation of nuclear reactors is ready to be built.

We can't wait that long to solve the climate crisis, not when there are better carbon-free energy sources ready to be used right now. Perhaps someday in the future, nuclear power can play a role in meeting our energy needs. In the meantime, we have to save our planet by choosing the solutions that will work today.

The Amazon is the largest rain forest on Earth, yet each year more than two million acres of it are destroyed.

CHAPTER 9

FORESTS: THE LUNGS OF THE WORLD

The world's forests are a mighty resource in the fight against the climate crisis. We must save them.

The world's forests are sometimes called "the lungs of the world." Every day, they take tons of carbon dioxide out of the air and give us back fresh oxygen to breathe. Yet we are thoughtlessly destroying this wonderful resource.

Deforestation—the destruction of the world's forests—is a major part of the climate crisis. Giant areas of forest are being cut down and burned every day. This hurts the climate in two ways: First, when the trees are burned, tons of carbon dioxide are released into the air. Second, the trees are no longer alive to take CO_2 out of the atmosphere.

The burning of forests around the world is the second biggest source of added CO_2 in the air. It is second only to the burning of fossil fuels.

About 22 percent of carbon dioxide pollution comes from the destruction of our forests. That's more than from all of the cars and trucks in the world.

SLASH-AND-BURN

Somewhere on the planet, slightly more than one acre of forest is being cut down every second. That adds up to almost 100,000 acres every day, or more than 34 million acres per year. Put together, that would make an area about the size of the state of Louisiana.

Most of this deforestation is happening in the developing nations of the tropics. This includes countries such as Brazil, Indonesia, Sudan, Myanmar, Zambia,

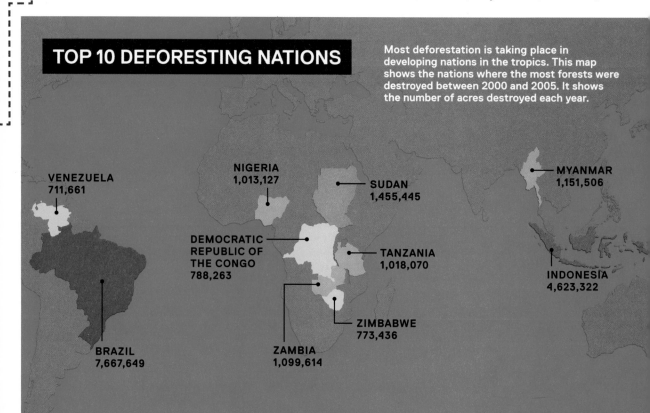

TOP 10 DEFORESTING NATIONS

Most deforestation is taking place in developing nations in the tropics. This map shows the nations where the most forests were destroyed between 2000 and 2005. It shows the number of acres destroyed each year.

VENEZUELA
711,661

NIGERIA
1,013,127

SUDAN
1,455,445

MYANMAR
1,151,506

DEMOCRATIC
REPUBLIC OF
THE CONGO
788,263

TANZANIA
1,018,070

INDONESIA
4,623,322

ZIMBABWE
773,436

BRAZIL
7,667,649

ZAMBIA
1,099,614

COUNTRIES WITH LARGEST NET LOSS OF FORESTS PER YEAR, 2000–2005 (acres/year)

Brazil is responsible for nearly half of all deforestation in the world. This portion of rain forest was burned to produce charcoal and open land for soybean and cattle farming.

Tanzania, and Nigeria. The first two, Brazil and Indonesia, are responsible for more than 60 percent of the deforestation in the world. Because of that, they are the third and fourth global warming polluters in the world, after China and the United States.

The forests are being destroyed mainly to make room for farms and ranches. Big ranchers and poor farmers alike are clearing trees at an alarming rate. The favorite method is called *slash-and-burn*. It works exactly like it sounds. First, the trees and other plants are cut down (slashed). Valuable wood is removed, and the rest is left to dry. Then the whole area is burned to clear it for farming.

Slash-and-burn farming is not new. It has been used for centuries by native people in the Amazon. It was used long ago by farmers in Europe. But today, large numbers of people are moving into the Amazon and other rain forests, like the Congo River basin in Africa. They are cutting down trees at a rate the world has never seen.

In Brazil, slash-and-burn has already destroyed 20 percent of the Amazon rain forest. Most of that land is being cleared for cattle. So not only are the trees gone, but they are being replaced with methane-producing cows, another cause of global warming.

Large areas of the last remaining peat swamp forest on Sumatra Island in Indonesia are being logged, burned, and drained to make way for palm oil plantations.

In Indonesia and nearby Malaysia, large forests are being cleared to make way for palm oil plantations. During the growing season in those countries, giant man-made fires burn down thousands of acres of trees. The fires also burn deep layers of carbon-rich peat moss in the forest floor. During those months, dark clouds of soot and smoke hang over southern Asia.

Palm oil (which comes from oil palm trees) is used as cooking oil. It can also be mixed with diesel fuel and burned in cars. (This kind of mixture is called *bio-diesel.*) It's true that when the oil palm trees are planted, they begin to absorb CO_2. However, old forests contain huge amounts of buried carbon. The new oil palm trees can never absorb all the CO_2 that was released when the old forest was burned.

WHO OWNS THE AMAZON?

Forests in these poorer countries are also

ROOM FOR TREES, APES, AND HUMANS

In 1989, Dr. Willie Smits saw a baby orangutan on a garbage heap in Balikpapan, Indonesia. The baby ape had "the saddest eyes I've ever seen," and she was very sick. Dr. Smits rescued her, nursed her back to health, and named her Uce.

Uce was just the start for Dr. Smits. Two years later, he founded the Borneo Orangutan Survival Foundation. Today it is the world's largest orangutan rescue project. The project's centers are home to more than 1,000 orangutan babies. But it has saved more than orangutans. Dr. Smits realized years ago that if he wanted to save the apes, he had to save the forest that is their home. Much of their habitat had been lost to deforestation.

To save the forest, Dr. Smits knew he had to enlist the help of the people who lived nearby. So Dr. Smits created something called a *conservation zone*. It is much more than a nature preserve. It is a way for local people to get income by preserving the forest. Then they have an economic reason to protect the orangutans' habitat.

In 2002, with the Masarang Foundation, he created a 5,000-acre forest reserve called Samboja Lestari ("Everlasting Forest"). The foundation replanted areas that had been deforested. Between the native trees, they planted crops of pineapples, papayas, and beans. Around the outer edge, they planted sugar palms. These crops are harvested by local people without cutting down trees. The sugar palms alone create jobs for 3,000 people.

Deep inside this reforested area, far from human populations, is the orangutan rescue center. Today, this reserve is home to more than 200 healthy orangutans. And reforestation seems to have reversed some climate trends. Air temperature has fallen 5.4–9°F, cloud cover has increased 11 percent, and rainfall is up 20 percent. The land, which had been reduced to desert, is now home to 1,800 species of trees, 137 bird species, and 30 species of reptiles.

"Everything is based upon that one thing—make sure that the forest remains there," says Dr. Smits. His aim is to put a value on the ecosystem high enough to keep it intact. "So if we want to help the orangutans—which I actually set out to do—we must make sure that the local people are the ones that benefit."

You can learn more about the Borneo Orangutan Survival Foundation at savetheorangutan.org, and about the Masarang Foundation at masarang.org.

Dr. Willie Smits with some of the orangutans his Borneo Orangutan Survival Foundation has helped.

being cleared to grow soybeans, sugarcane, and many other cash crops. Many people in these nations live in extreme poverty. The lure of making some money from these crops is just too hard to resist. Governments sometimes help with the clearing of forests. Or, if the forests are supposed to be protected, governments often look the other way.

This is a difficult problem. The fact is that when the nations of Europe and North America were developing, we cut down many of our forests. Before European settlement, the United States was covered in trees from the Atlantic Ocean to the Mississippi River. Now we are telling the poorer nations of the world that because of the climate crisis, they may not do the same thing.

Nations like Brazil, Indonesia, and the Democratic Republic of the Congo resent this. They feel they must develop their economies and help their people out of poverty. They feel they have the right to decide what to do with their own resources. This sometimes makes them resist outside efforts to protect their forests.

We may feel the Amazon rain forest belongs to the world, but the people of Brazil have every right to improve their lives with the resources in their country. The answer lies in showing people how they can make more money by protecting and saving their forests.

There are a few things that can help us make this argument. First, the soil in tropical rain forests isn't very good for farming. Surprisingly, it is usually thin and not very fertile. Turning it into farmland doesn't really make economic sense.

We must also convince people that the rain forest can be a much greater resource if it is left standing.

One reason for this is *biodiversity*. That simply means that the rain forests are home to a huge number of different (diverse) plants and animals. More than 50 percent of all the known species on Earth are found in tropical forests. And no one knows how many undiscovered species may be there. These species are a great source for new medicines and new foods, any one of which could mean new income for those countries. But if we destroy the forests, we'll never know exactly what we have lost.

If you look at this eroded riverbank in the Amazon, you can see a line of brown soil just under the trees. The fertile soil in a rain forest is often just that very thin layer. That's why rain forests do not make good cropland.

THE COST OF DEFORESTATION

To many people, turning forests into farmland seems like a good way to make money. This is because they do not measure the true value of forests. Calculating the real worth of a forest is

only possible when we know the cost of putting more carbon into the air.

How do we calculate the price of carbon? By calculating the cost of the damage that the climate crisis is doing to our economy and our environment. Then we could charge polluters a fee for every ton of CO_2 they put into our air. (This is

THE SIXTH GREAT EXTINCTION

Most biologists believe that we are now in a time of mass extinction. That means that large numbers of species are disappearing at the same time. One big cause is the destruction of tropical rain forests, which are habitats for so many plants and animals. The last great extinction occurred when a giant asteroid hit the earth 65 million years ago, wiping out many species on Earth, including the dinosaurs.

Among the best-known species now at risk are the orangutan in Borneo, the Sumatran tiger, the Asian elephant, and our closest relatives, the chimpanzees and gorillas of Africa.

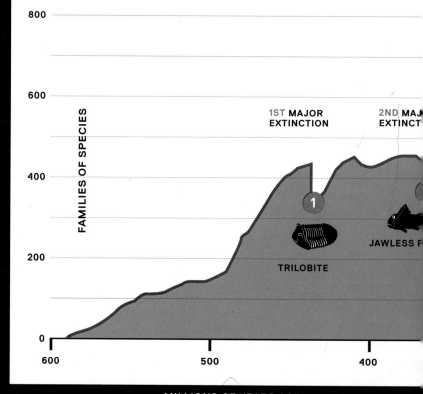

This graph shows the number of families of species over time, based on the fossil record. A species family is a group of animals that are closely related. Each big dip in the graph marks another major extinction. The illustrations show examples of some of the animals that went extinct at each point.

FAMILIES OF SPECIES

800

600

1ST MAJOR EXTINCTION

2ND MAJOR EXTINCTION

400

1

JAWLESS F

TRILOBITE

200

0

600   500   400

MILLIONS OF YEARS AGO

explained in greater detail in Chapter 15.)

Once you figure out the true cost of carbon dioxide pollution, cutting down a forest does not make much sense. Suppose you clear 2.5 acres of forest in a country like Brazil. You might be able to sell that land for $300. But cutting down and burning those trees will release 500 tons of CO_2 into the air. If you were charged a fair carbon tax, say about $30 a ton, clearing that field would cost you $15,000.

This kind of carbon tax has to be applied to *all* forests in the world. That is the best way to get people everywhere to start protecting and preserving them.

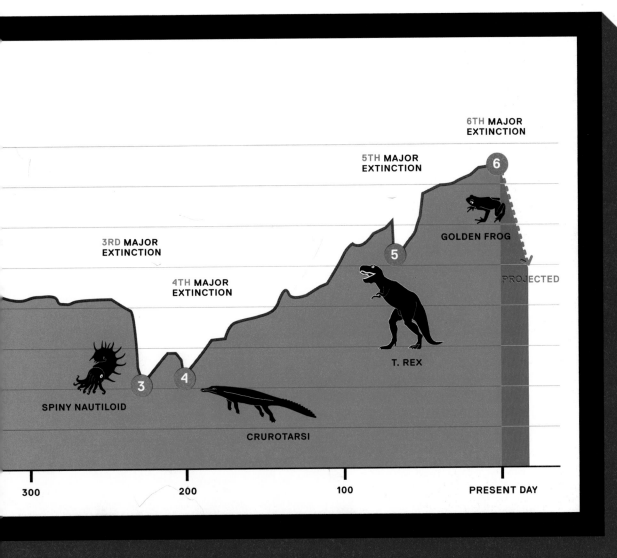

6TH **MAJOR EXTINCTION**

5TH **MAJOR EXTINCTION**

3RD **MAJOR EXTINCTION**

4TH **MAJOR EXTINCTION**

GOLDEN FROG

PROJECTED

T. REX

SPINY NAUTILOID

CRUROTARSI

300   200   100   PRESENT DAY

CAN FORESTS SURVIVE?

Even as we look to forests to help us fight the climate crisis, many forests are dying—because of global warming. As temperatures rise, the change in climate is weakening some trees and making it possible for pests and disease to kill them.

For example, forests in Canada and the United States are dying because of an invasion of mountain pine beetles. The beetles tunnel into the bark of the trees, killing them. Cold winter weather used to kill off enough beetles to keep them in check. This is no longer true. Also, longer and more frequent droughts weaken the trees, making it easier for the beetles to attack.

More than 30 million acres of Canadian forests and more than seven million acres

Winters have not been cold enough to kill off mountain pine beetles in Colorado. More than 600,000 acres of forest in Colorado are now affected by the pest.

WANGARI MAATHAI: A NOBEL PEACE PRIZE FOR TREES

How can one woman plant 30 million trees? Wangari Maathai did it by starting a movement. The organization she founded in 1977, called the Green Belt Movement, has worked ever since to plant trees in her native Kenya, as well as in 11 other African countries. But the goals of the movement go way beyond tree planting. The trees are part of a broader program to fight poverty, develop agriculture, and enable people to take control of their communities and their lives.

Maathai was awarded the Nobel Peace Prize in 2004. Today, she is working with the United Nations on its program "Plant for the Planet: Billion Tree Campaign." The program has already planted more than three billion trees around the world.

You can read more about Wangari Maathai and the Green Belt Movement at greenbeltmovement.org.

---

in the U.S. have been hurt by this pest. Evergreen forests throughout North America and Europe are facing invasions of similar beetles.

Some have argued that rising CO_2 levels will make trees and plants grow faster. This is partly true. Some plants will grow faster with more carbon. However, there is a natural limit to how fast plants can grow. Meanwhile, the harmful effects of drought, wildfire, and disease will wipe out any small benefits from extra CO_2.

SAVE THE TREES

We should not forget that forests do a lot more for us besides gather carbon dioxide. They protect against soil erosion and help store water in the soil. As we've noted, forests are an important home to wildlife. When carefully managed, they can provide income to people and wood products to society. For all of these reasons, we need to preserve what's left of the world's forests. It is not too late. In

just the past few years, people in every nation have come to recognize just how important this is.

Saving the forests means making a deal between the industrialized countries and the developing countries. We must give them the aid they need to find other paths to development. With this aid, they can build carbon-free economies. And they can find ways to make money from their forests without cutting them down. That includes replanting trees in many areas.

Governments around the world are beginning to make serious efforts to protect their forests. For example, Brazil has a goal of reducing deforestation by 70 percent by the year 2017. China halted all deforestation 10 years ago. Today, it is a leader in replanting trees, or *reforestation*.

The Chinese people planted about 12 million acres of forests in 2008 alone. They even passed a law that says all citizens over the age of 11 have a duty to plant three trees a year. In Chinese schools, each student must plant at least one tree before graduating.

Planting a tree may not seem like much, but it's one of the most direct things you can do to fight the climate crisis.

▶ **If each person in the world planted two seedlings a year for 10 years, it would make up for all the deforestation of the past 10 years.**

Young people around the world have taken up tree planting as a simple and powerful way to fight global warming.

REASONS FOR HOPE

There are other reasons for hope. There has been a rapid growth of environmental groups in developing countries. These groups are tackling all sorts of environmental issues, not just the climate crisis. They are working with local governments to develop detailed plans for saving their trees and planting new ones. And thanks to new satellite technology, we can now keep track of the world's forests. Photos taken from space can tell us if deforestation is taking place anywhere in the world. In some areas, the photos are so good that we can keep track of forests tree by tree!

But it will take more than satellite photos to save our forests. People of all nations must work together to save this amazing resource. If we do, we will all be able to breathe a little easier.

Soil is like the living "skin" of the earth. Here, a scientist studies the soil in Washington State's Palouse River Basin, which has suffered from erosion.

CHAPTER 10

We can build healthy soils and farmland by taking some of the extra carbon out of the air and putting it back in the dirt.

One cause of the climate crisis is too much carbon in the air. But there's another crisis related to global warming, and it's happening in the ground beneath our feet. It's a crisis of the soil, a crisis caused by too *little* carbon.

In the air, carbon is found in compounds like carbon dioxide and methane. In the ground, it's fixed in other compounds, like carbohydrates, especially in the roots, leaves, and stems of plants. But it's all the same element—carbon.

In the past, the carbon cycle balanced the carbon in the air and the carbon in the plants and soil. Now that cycle is out of balance, thanks to the burning of fossil fuels and other human activity. There's too much carbon in the air and, in many places, not enough carbon in the soil.

DOWN IN THE DIRT

Too much carbon in the air is heating up our climate. But without enough carbon in the soil, plants cannot grow.

We need to take the extra carbon out of the air and put it in the ground, where it can make healthy, fertile soil and help feed the world.

If we do this, we can help solve the climate crisis and the soil crisis at the same time. This is another choice we must make.

THE LIVING SOIL

As a boy, I spent summers on my family's farm in Tennessee. I learned from my father that the most fertile soil is a deep, rich black. But it was not until much later in my life that I learned the reason fertile soil is black: it's the carbon.

Much of the carbon comes from the remains of dead plants. When they are alive, the plants take carbon out of the air and out of the soil. When they die, they decay, and the carbon goes back into the air and the soil.

Have you ever seen an old, wet pile of leaves? The leaves at the bottom are turning black and decaying. They are on their way to becoming part of the soil.

Rich black soil, also called *humus*, is about 58 percent carbon. The rest is made up of other important elements, like nitrogen and minerals, that plants need to grow. Fertile soil is also filled with bacteria, fungi, worms, insects, and other living organisms.

If forests are the lungs of the world, then the soil is its skin. To grow our food, we need living, breathing soil, full of carbon, nitrogen, and all the microbes and animals that help plants grow.

THE SOIL CRISIS

You might wonder how there can be a soil crisis. After all, isn't there dirt everywhere in the world? How can we run out of soil? The problem is, not all soil is good for growing crops. Some places have deep, carbon-rich soil. In other areas, the soil has very little carbon. That can make it impossible to grow food.

INSIDE OUR SOIL

Fertile soil is full of life. It contains bacteria, fungi, worms, insects, and other animals. It is made of a rich mixture of dead plant matter, minerals, and other important nutrients. All of these things are necessary for healthy plants to grow.

HUMUS

FUNGI

BACTERIA

115

Some of the world's worst soil erosion can be seen in the Loess Plateau in Shaanxi province, China. Only small fields for crops remain as the land is stripped away.

The soil of the earth holds a lot of carbon, more than twice as much carbon as the atmosphere. Most of that carbon is found in just the first few inches of soil, the *topsoil*. But fertile topsoil is not spread evenly. In some places it has been built up over centuries. In other places it has washed away and been lost. In many areas of the world, poor farming methods are causing a giant loss of topsoil. This is the *soil crisis*. There are several ways that farming can destroy topsoil. One way is by too much plowing. Plowing means digging into the soil and turning it over. Farmers plow mainly to get rid of weeds and to make it easier to plant seeds. But plowing also digs up the carbon-rich topsoil. This releases a lot of carbon into the air and makes the soil less fertile.

Another way farmers lose topsoil is by planting in the wrong place. If a farmer

cuts down the trees on a hillside and plows a field, he might get a year or two of crops. But the roots of the trees kept the topsoil in place. Without the trees, the hillside will soon become bare. The soil will be lost through erosion, washed away by rain, or blown away by wind.

When a crop is harvested, farmers often leave part of the plant in the field. They take the grain or vegetable and leave the stems and leaves. These remains of the plants rot, and their carbon goes back into the soil. In poorer countries, however, people often remove every single bit of the plants. That means the soil loses more carbon every year.

THE AMERICAN DUST BOWL

In the 1930s, when my father was a young man, there was a soil crisis in the United States. Across the Midwest and the West, in places like Kansas and Iowa, soil erosion was destroying farmland.

The farms in the American Midwest and West were built on the Great Plains. These were grasslands that had never been plowed before European settlers arrived. The soil in the plains had been built up over centuries. It was fertilized by the manure of giant herds of buffalo that grazed on the grasses. In some places, the topsoil was four feet deep.

Farmers loved the thick black earth of the plains. They didn't realize that as they plowed it, they were losing the carbon that made the land so fertile. Huge amounts of carbon were released

A father and sons in Oklahoma in 1936. The environmental disaster of the Dust Bowl was brought on by drought and farming practices that did not protect against erosion.

into the air. Plowing made the soil looser, and without the roots of the grasses to hold the topsoil year-round, the soil began to erode and blow away. Giant dust storms darkened the sky. The American plains had been home to some of the most fertile farmland in the world. Now the area became known as the Dust Bowl.

To this day, I remember the lessons my father taught me, lessons that came from the days of the Dust Bowl. For example, when walking across the farm, watch for the first hint of erosion; stop it before it takes away a whole field or a whole farm. There were other lessons, too. For example, American farmers no longer plow the way they used to. And they leave the remains of the crops in the field to decay and nourish the soil.

Sadly, the lessons of the American Dust Bowl are not being followed in the rest of the world. This is especially true in Africa, where poor farming methods are destroying soil quality in large areas. More than 80 percent of the farmland in Africa is at risk. This loss of soil is threatening the food supply of millions of people. These farming methods also release even more carbon into the air, adding to global warming.

PUTTING THE CARBON BACK

This all adds up to some big problems. In fact, there are really three different, but connected, problems:

1. Soil erosion in developing countries threatens the food supply.

2. Modern agriculture, by using fossil fuels, adds to the climate crisis.

3. The climate crisis is already hurting the world's food supply.

The good news is that all three of these problems have the same solution. We have to stop putting carbon into the air and instead put it into the ground. If we choose to do this, we can protect the topsoil, end our use of fossil fuels in farming, and help stop global warming all at the same time.

One way to do this is to support organic farming. Organic farmers do

FARMS IN TROUBLE

Global warming is already having a serious effect on the world's farms. It is shifting weather patterns, causing some areas to get a lot more rain while others get less. Heat waves and droughts can kill plants and add to soil erosion. When it's hot, plants need more water, and some plants just cannot grow when the temperature is too high. Warmer weather often means more insects, which can destroy crops in the fields.

These changes in climate are already causing a severe farm crisis in countries close to the equator. If we do nothing about global warming, countries like India, Mexico, and Sudan will see their crops cut by as much as 50 percent.

Modern farms, which often grow just one variety of one plant, can be especially hard hit by changes in the climate. If the temperature gets too high for that one plant, then the farmer has no other source of income.

It's true, as we mentioned in Chapter 9, that increased CO_2 levels help some plants to grow. However, it turns out the plants that do best with more carbon dioxide are weeds. They grow faster, and weed killers don't work as well on them. (By the way, one of the weeds that does really well with more CO_2 is poison ivy. It doesn't just grow faster; its poison gets stronger.)

This threat to agriculture is one of the most serious problems caused by global warming. It's another reason we must act swiftly to halt this crisis.

Record-breaking drought and heat in Australia have been a disaster for the country's farms. These apples have been sunburned on their trees.

A father and his son work on an organic farm in Whatcom County, Washington. Organic farming has been proven to increase the carbon content of soil.

not use artificial fertilizers or herbicides. They rely on manure, crop rotation, and other solar-based practices. This produces fertile, living, carbon-rich topsoil. Organic farms use fewer fossil fuels, and their natural soil produces healthier food. And if the organic farm is local, it uses less energy to transport the food from the farm to your table.

Organic food is the fastest-growing part of U.S. agriculture. That's because consumers like you and me have chosen to buy organic meats, fruits, and vegetables. We know that even if they cost a few pennies more, in the long run they are really much cheaper. They are healthier for us, and they do not

add to global warming. Buying organic food is one of the simplest, most direct choices we can make. At every meal, we have the chance to vote against the climate crisis and for the environment.

Right now, the U.S. government spends billions of taxpayer dollars to support big industrial farms that use artificial fertilizer, herbicide, and pesticide. Our government spends very little to support organic farming. This is the opposite of what we should be doing. Just as we should tax carbon polluters, we should give tax breaks to farmers who don't release carbon into the air but capture it in their fields. That would quickly put modern agriculture on the right track.

In West Virginia, a poultry farmer produces biochar from chicken waste and wood chips, turning it into a valuable fertilizer.

BIOCHAR

Organic farming will cut global warming pollution, but it won't capture a lot of extra carbon dioxide that is in the air. To do that, we need to use something called *biochar.*

Biochar is short for biological charcoal. As you may know, charcoal is mostly carbon. Biochar is a form of charcoal that does not decay or break down in most soils. That means biochar, buried in the ground, will hold most of its carbon for up to 1,000 years.

Not only that, but biochar is porous, which means that water can flow through it. It's an excellent home for fungi, bacteria, and other organisms that make healthy soil. So putting biochar in the ground not only buries carbon, it also makes the soil more fertile.

This is not a new invention. Scientists recently discovered deep layers of biochar in parts of the Amazon rain forest. The charcoal was put there at least 1,000 years ago by Indian farmers. They buried charcoal and broken pottery in the ground and created very fertile fields. This soil is called *terra preta*, which means "black earth" in Portuguese. (Portuguese is the main language of Brazil.) Even today, this *terra preta* soil is much more fertile than surrounding soils.

Biochar can be made from weeds, crop remains, wood, or even manure—just about anything that was once a living plant. And there is a way to make it that releases no carbon dioxide. So here's the solution to the soil crisis and a big part of ending the climate crisis:

Plants capture carbon from the air, and we turn the plants into biochar. Then we bury the biochar in the ground, where it builds healthy, fertile soil.

There are ways of making biochar in simple stoves that can be used anywhere. Biochar can be used in the developing world as well as on modern, industrial farms.

Biochar is a way to take large amounts of carbon out of the air quite quickly— if we choose to do it.

FERTILE FARMS FROM CARBON

Our farms and our food supply are in trouble. But we already know the answer—put the carbon back in the soil and keep it there where it can help grow crops. If we do this, agriculture can help stop global warming instead of causing it. Scientists think that if we change the way we farm, farmland can absorb about 15 percent of global warming pollution. We can save topsoil around the world and create new, fertile topsoil—without burning fossil fuels.

This will help people in every nation around the world, rich and poor alike. After all, everyone needs healthy food, and so everyone needs healthy soil. And we can have both—if we choose.

The busy Oshodi Market in Lagos, the largest city in Nigeria.

CHAPTER 11

NINE BILLION NEIGHBORS

Part of the solution to the climate crisis is slowing population growth until it levels off a few decades from now.

People often ask me if the climate crisis is caused by the huge growth in world population. The answer is that population growth is part of the problem. The world population grew from 1.6 billion people in 1900 to almost 6.8 billion today. All those extra people consume goods and use energy—which means more fossil fuels burned and more global warming.

And the world's population is still growing. There will be about one billion more people on the planet before the year 2025. Most of those extra people will live in less-developed countries. As the economies in those nations grow, their residents will want the same things that the inhabitants of industrialized nations have: cars, television sets, washing machines, etc. And that means we will need even more energy.

The good news is that the world's population growth is slowing down.

Scientists think it will reach about 9.1 billion and then stabilize. The planet should be able to support that many people—if we change the way we live by cutting global warming pollution and by learning to consume a little less. But like global warming, population growth won't stop by itself. It's up to us to make sure it does.

A SUCCESS STORY

It might surprise you to learn this: in terms of population growth, we are seeing a historic success story. Thirty years ago, scientists talked about the "ticking time bomb" of population growth. Today, human population growth is slowing down dramatically. It's happening in slow motion, but the slowdown is very real.

There are a lot of reasons for this, and they are all connected. To put it very simply, people in poorer nations, where there is a high death rate, choose to have more children. As nations become more industrial, as people earn higher incomes and receive more education, and as the people live longer, they choose to have fewer children.

It may seem strange that as the death rate goes down in a country, so does population growth. After all, if people are living longer, doesn't that mean there will be more people? It turns out the opposite happens. If people know their children will survive until adulthood, they will choose to have fewer kids. The slowdown in the birthrate more than makes up for the slowdown in the death rate. As a result, the population stops growing as quickly and can even begin to shrink.

A.D. 1 50 100 150 200 250 300 350 400 450 500 550 600 650 700 750 800 850 900 950 1000

POPULATION GROWTH

As the world's population has grown, so has the CO_2 entering the air.
The two are related, but they don't always exactly match. It was only
after we began burning fossil fuels that CO_2 levels climbed much faster.

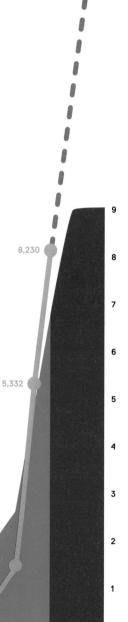

15,000

9
8,230
8
7
6
5,332
5
4
3
2
1,630
1
0

BILLIONS OF PEOPLE

ANNUAL CARBON EMISSIONS
(in million metric tons)

PROJECTED ANNUAL CARBON EMISSIONS ("business as usual" model)
(in million metric tons)

RECORDED POPULATION

PROJECTED POPULATION

1200 1250 1300 1350 1400 1450 1500 1550 1600 1650 1700 1750 1800 1850 1900 1950 2000 2050 2100

THE BIG SHIFT

That is exactly what is happening today. Thanks to changes in the global economy, and because of decisions made by political leaders, the population explosion is beginning to slow down. Because of the fall in birthrates, around the year 2050, the world population should stop growing.

This is only partly because of improving health and survival rates. For example, families that work on farms need lots of hands to work the land. But if more families live and work in cities, they don't have the same need for large families. Also, for children to succeed in an industrial nation, they must go further in school and perhaps to college. That takes a lot more time and money—another reason to have fewer children.

Scientists have been studying these changes in population growth. They've discovered that it's not as simple as rising income or industrial development. It turns out there are four factors that work together to slow birthrates in developing nations. They are:

▶▶ FOUR FACTORS TO SLOW POPULATION GROWTH

1. EDUCATION FOR GIRLS

A primary school class in Pakistan

2. EQUAL RIGHTS FOR WOMEN

Women voting in Iran

1. The widespread education of girls.
2. Equal rights for women, allowing them to participate in the decisions of their families, communities, and nations.
3. Better health systems that lead to high child-survival rates. This makes parents feel confident that most or all of their children will survive into adulthood.
4. The ability of women to choose how many children they will have and when they will have them.

The good news is that there is a lot of proof this works. These four factors, if they happen at the same time, lead to smaller families and slower population growth. This shift is happening in every nation in the world.

In fact, in 44 out of the 45 most developed nations with populations over 100,000, the birthrate is now so low that more people are dying than being born. The only reason the population in most of these countries doesn't shrink is because of new immigrants from other countries. Some poor countries will continue to have high birthrates for some time, but the rate is dropping.

3. HIGH CHILD-SURVIVAL RATES

4. WOMEN CHOOSE WHEN TO HAVE BABIES AND HOW MANY THEY WILL HAVE

A measles vaccination in Tajikistan

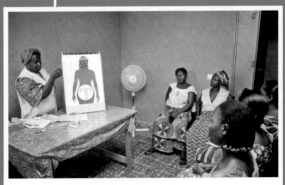

A family planning clinic in Ivory Coast

GROWING CITIES, GROWING PROBLEMS

This news is a great source of hope. At the same time, as poor countries become richer, they face a new problem: *urbanization*. That simply means the growth of urban areas. Around the world, small cities are becoming big cities, and big cities are becoming huge ones. There are fewer jobs on farms, and people have to move to the city to find work. For the first time in human history, more people live in cities than in the countryside.

Lagos, the largest city in Nigeria, has grown from 1.9 million people in 1975 to 9.5 million in 2007. It might reach 15.8 million in 2025. Kinshasa, the capital of the Democratic Republic of the Congo, is the fastest-growing city in the world.

THE GROWTH OF MEGACITIES

For the first time in human history, more than half the world's population lives in cities. By 2025, there will be as many as 27 *megacities* in the world. (A megacity is an urban area with more than 10 million people.)

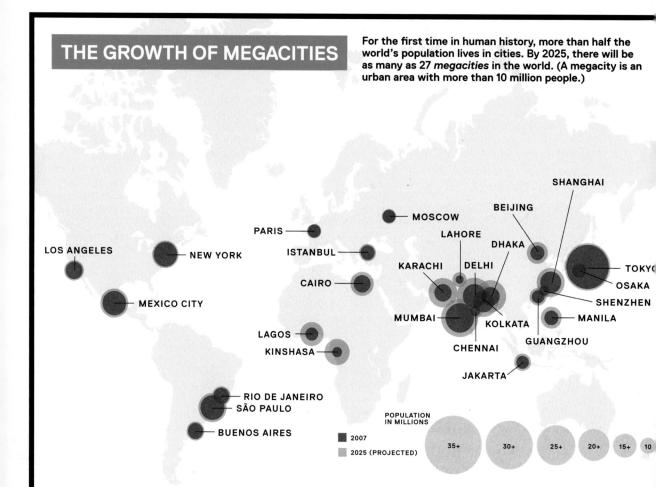

LOS ANGELES
NEW YORK
MEXICO CITY
PARIS
ISTANBUL
CAIRO
MOSCOW
LAHORE
KARACHI
DELHI
DHAKA
BEIJING
SHANGHAI
TOKYO
OSAKA
SHENZHEN
MANILA
MUMBAI
KOLKATA
GUANGZHOU
CHENNAI
JAKARTA
LAGOS
KINSHASA
RIO DE JANEIRO
SÃO PAULO
BUENOS AIRES

POPULATION IN MILLIONS

■ 2007
■ 2025 (PROJECTED)

35+   30+   25+   20+   15+   10

People scramble to get water from a water truck in a poor neighborhood of Delhi, India. This slum is home to 4,000 workers but has no clean water supply.

With 7.8 million people in 2007, it is expected to have 16.8 million in 2025. Many of these growing cities are in coastal areas—exactly the places that are threatened by the rising sea levels caused by global warming.

The rapid spread of urban areas puts a lot of pressure on the environment. For example, many cities around the world face a shrinking water supply. Their pipelines are old and leaking. Diseases like cholera sometimes infect the water supply. Mexico City is the largest city in the Americas and is growing every year. In 2009, there was less rainfall than normal. The city ran out of water and had to cut off the supply to hundreds of thousands of people.

As people move into cities, they start using more energy. Around the globe, as people earn higher incomes, one of the first things they do is buy a car. The world's urban areas suffer from massive traffic jams, smog, and increased CO_2 pollution. Right now it seems as though our cities are built for cars, not people. But cities do not have to be energy hogs. If we plan our cities around mass transit—subways, buses, and trains—then the growing cities do not have to be a threat to the planet.

There is no guarantee that the world's population growth will slow down. It will only happen if governments everywhere continue to support the four factors mentioned earlier. This can be a difficult thing to discuss in some countries. It involves talking about the rights of women and also about family planning. However, it is also one of the rare subjects on which most political leaders agree. And it is one area in which the world community has a proven track record of success.

The most powerful thing we can do is make sure that girls everywhere are educated. We may take that for granted in the United States, but in many countries, there are still few schools girls can attend. When there are schools for girls, families often do not want to send them, thinking it a waste of time and money.

Recent experience has shown that when girls are well-educated in large numbers, it has a strong impact on many other issues.

Young women learn about biology at a Muslim boarding school in Indonesia.

Educated girls grow up to be educated women who voice their opinions and take part in the life of their communities and their countries.

They often delay the age at which they marry. They start making well-informed decisions about when and if they will have children. They work for better child and health care, which raises child-survival rates.

For example, Saudi Arabia used to have one of the highest population growth rates in the world. Today, 55 percent of college graduates there are women. And sure enough, the population growth rate in the country has been slowing. The average number of children in a family 30 years ago was 7.3; now it's 3.2.

The worldwide communications revolution—satellite television, the Internet, and cell phone technology—seems to have speeded up the movement toward more education for girls. Modern technology allows girls to see examples of educated and independent women. This can inspire them to seek out education for themselves.

OUR JOB

Developing countries are already facing huge problems. Some are due to population growth. Some are political problems like civil war and other conflicts. All of their systems—including their economies, health care, and education—are stretched to the breaking point.

Although most industrialized nations do give aid to poorer nations, there is a lot more we can do. We have to find ways to promote sustainable economic development worldwide. We also must support the policies that help slow population growth, like equal rights for women and education for girls.

Remember, when we talk about the number of people in the world, that includes us. We are all in this together and we must act together to save our home, the earth. There is enough room on this planet for everyone—if we act now.

Turbines convert different kinds of power, like steam or wind, into electricity. But old-model turbines lose or waste a lot of energy. New, more efficient turbines like this one do a much better job.

CHAPTER 12

SAVE ENERGY AND SAVE THE PLANET

The easiest way to fight global warming is to use less energy.

There is a very simple way to cut global warming pollution, and it's something anyone can do. We just have to use less energy. Cutting back on energy use means we can burn less coal and oil. And that means we produce less carbon dioxide and other greenhouse gases.

It will take time to build new solar, wind, and geothermal power plants. But we can cut back on energy use today. And we can cut back on energy use even without making big changes in the way we live. The trick is to use energy more *efficiently*.

135

enough power to be able to sell some to other countries.

BETTER BUILDINGS

When we do heat our homes and buildings, we have to make sure we aren't wasting energy there also. Every time we can save energy, we lower our costs, cut fuel use, and fight global warming.

Right now, 30 to 40 percent of our CO_2 emissions are created just to make heat that is lost from buildings. That means all of that carbon is going into the air to make energy *that we're not even using.*

Appliances with an Energy Star rating are more efficient and help people save money on their electricity bills.

The solution is simple: we have to insulate our buildings, our homes, schools, offices, stores—all of them.

(*Insulation* is material in the walls of buildings that keeps heat in—or out in the summer.)

One thing we must do is change the building codes. Those are the laws that tell builders how much insulation they must put into new buildings. The codes should be updated to make sure builders are using the best, most efficient insulation methods. We must also make it possible for homeowners to get low-cost loans to pay for new insulation in old buildings. These changes to old homes usually pay for themselves in three years because of savings in energy bills.

We also have to change what's inside our buildings. We've seen that many industrial motors and machines are inefficient. So are many home heating systems and appliances. These should either be repaired or replaced with new, more efficient models. The

HOT

COOL

The white and red areas in this photo show where heat energy is leaking out of the house. Roofs and window frames are often the most wasteful areas in a home.

Department of Energy rates new appliances like refrigerators and air conditioners. Those that have been given an Energy Star rating are the most efficient and will offer the most savings on electricity bills. They also give Energy Star ratings to new homes that meet high efficiency standards.

While we're making our buildings more efficient, we should also work on our cities. Large cities are already pretty energy efficient. In cities, it's easier for people to get around by walking or riding bicycles. Buses and trains and other types of mass transportation are much more energy efficient than cars. Apartment buildings are better at keeping heat in than individual homes. But we can do much better.

We have to begin thinking of our cities as energy systems.

Once we find the places where those systems are losing energy, we can

---

 ## IS YOUR TELEVISION REALLY OFF?

Can you save electricity by turning off your television set? Not as much as you think. When you press "off," most modern TVs, DVD players, and other electronic devices don't really shut off. They go into a standby mode. That means they are still using electricity. Those blinking lights and digital clocks are still using energy.

In the same way, when your computer goes to "sleep," it's still using electricity. Many people leave their computers in sleep mode all night long so they won't have to wait a few seconds for them to come on in the morning. Computer printers also use electricity all the time, even when they are not printing.

This adds up to a giant waste of electricity. For example, the electricity being burned just by U.S. television sets that are "off" would equal the output of an entire power plant. The worst offenders are DVRs—the digital television recorders many people now use.

Even when it is "off," a DVR can use 50 watts of power. That's like leaving a lightbulb on 24 hours a day.

Televisions and printers and DVRs are designed this way to make them easier to use. But they can be designed differently. Electronics companies must redesign their products to use much less electricity, especially when they are not being used. Then we won't have to wonder if we have really turned them off or not.

A special lane for buses in Jakarta, Indonesia, allows mass-transit riders to speed past cars during rush hour.

begin to fix the leaks, saving money and the environment at the same time.

A MILLION SOLUTIONS

Saving energy isn't very dramatic. We can't point to one thing and say we've found the solution. Instead, there are millions of solutions. Almost anywhere we look we can find ways to save energy. That's the beauty of it. Because once we start training ourselves to look, we are going to find a million new ways to do it. And once people see that each solution will save them money, they will begin looking all the time.

The other advantage to saving energy is that everyone can do it. Big companies can save energy, and so can individuals. Young people can change a lightbulb, help with the recycling, or turn off their computers instead of putting them to sleep.

So we all have to get to work, saving money while saving energy. It's the best way to save our planet.

A worker in a tangle of wires in Shanghai, China. We need a new system to manage and deliver electricity.

CHAPTER 13

A SUPERHIGHWAY FOR ELECTRICITY

We need a new system to transport and store electricity—one designed for renewable energy sources.

We don't usually think about electricity—we just flip a switch and it's there, in the wires in our home. But how does the electric current get there?

You've probably seen tall power lines running alongside a highway or through your town. Those lines are part of a giant electricity network or *grid*. The grid is a complex system that transports the electricity from power plants to homes, schools, and businesses. It includes high-voltage lines, local power stations, and all the smaller cables that carry electricity to consumers.

The electric grid we have in the U.S. was built piece by piece during the 20th century. When it was new, it was a marvel of engineering and technology. But today, it's out of date and wastes electricity. What's more, our electric grid was not built to handle solar, wind, or geothermal power.

If we are to switch our country to renewable energy sources, we will need a new electric grid—one built for the 21st century.

We need a "smarter" grid, one that uses the latest computer technology. Building a new, smart grid is one of the challenges we must meet if we are going to stop the climate crisis.

DELIVERING THE POWER

In the 1950s, the U.S. government decided to build a nationwide network of highways for cars and trucks. That became the Interstate Highway System. Later, in the 1980s and '90s, new technology was used to build a worldwide information superhighway—which became the Internet. Now we must build a superhighway for electricity.

At the Department of Energy's Rocky Mountain office, power system dispatchers distribute hydroelectricity throughout the western United States.

Our present electric grid is built around large power plants that generate electricity around the clock. But solar- and wind-powered plants do not. This creates a problem for the engineers who run our grid. For example, the Bonneville Power Administration supplies electricity to the Pacific Northwest. When the wind is blowing, it gets about 2,000 megawatts of electricity from wind turbines. That's enough for two cities the size of Seattle. But when the wind stops, that power is gone.

And it's not just renewable energy that can be unreliable. The present grid already has trouble keeping up with demand, especially during peak hours. For example, on summer days there is a lot of demand in some cities because of air conditioning.

Some of the technology in the present grid is 100 years old. When overloaded, it sometimes fails, causing power outages or blackouts. Problems with electric supply, like blackouts and power surges, cause businesses to lose billions of dollars.

In August 2003, the largest blackout in North American history affected more than 50 million people, including all of New York City.

(A power surge is when the voltage in a line suddenly spikes. This can damage electronic equipment like computers.) Some experts think problems with the present grid cost us more than $200 billion a year.

A grid with 21st century technology would be able to smooth out the ups and downs of electricity from solar and wind sources. It would be able to adjust to peak demand hours and shift power from one region to another, depending on which plants are operating. It would be a truly national grid, unlike the present one that was pieced together, region by region, as it grew.

NEW POWER LINES

Many new solar and wind power sources are far from existing power lines. We will have to build new high-voltage power lines to reach them.

Voltage is one way of measuring the strength of an electric current. (You can think of voltage as something like the pressure of the electricity, like the water pressure in a pipe.) The electric current in homes in the United States is 110 volts. But the electricity in high-voltage power lines can be up to 750,000 volts! The high voltage makes it possible to transmit electricity over long distances.

With new technology, we can build power lines that carry even bigger loads—more than 760 kilovolts. (A *kilovolt* is a thousand volts.) All electric lines lose some of the energy they carry. But the new higher-voltage lines are much more efficient and lose less energy than the lines they replace. So if we replace all of our old power lines with new ones, we will actually save money by saving electricity.

And there could be another benefit to building new power lines. Many of the new lines will be buried in the ground. With the right planning, we could lay down fiber-optic broadband cables and increase our Internet connections at the same time.

GET SMART

The new grid will be more efficient because it will use computer technology. That's why it's sometimes called a "smart" grid. Software in the system will be able to spot trouble before blackouts can occur. It will tell managers where repairs are needed and reroute the flow of electricity to avoid any loss of power.

A smart grid will make it possible for power companies to charge consumers different rates at different times of the day. This is important for reducing peak electricity use. For example, power companies would like to get people to use appliances like washing machines at night, when demand is lower. If electricity was cheaper at night, you could choose to run your washing machine then and save money.

Peak and off-peak power will be just one of the choices you'll be able to make. With a smart grid, an electricity bill will look more like a cell phone bill. You'll be able to set a limit on how much you want to pay each month. Then you'll pick from different services, the way you pick different cell phone plans today.

STORING ELECTRICITY

One of the biggest changes we need in our power grid is a good way to store large amounts of electricity. As we've noted, solar and wind power are *intermittent*. That means they start and stop. We need a way to store electricity while those power sources are running so we can use it when they are not.

Electric storage would also solve the

 COLD STORAGE

One really cool way to store energy is with ice. The Bank of America Tower in New York City makes more than a half a million pounds of ice every night. Then the ice is used to cool the buildings the next day. Not only is this cheaper than running regular air-conditioning during the day, it shifts electricity demand from peak to off-peak hours. With electric rates lower at night, the savings are even greater.

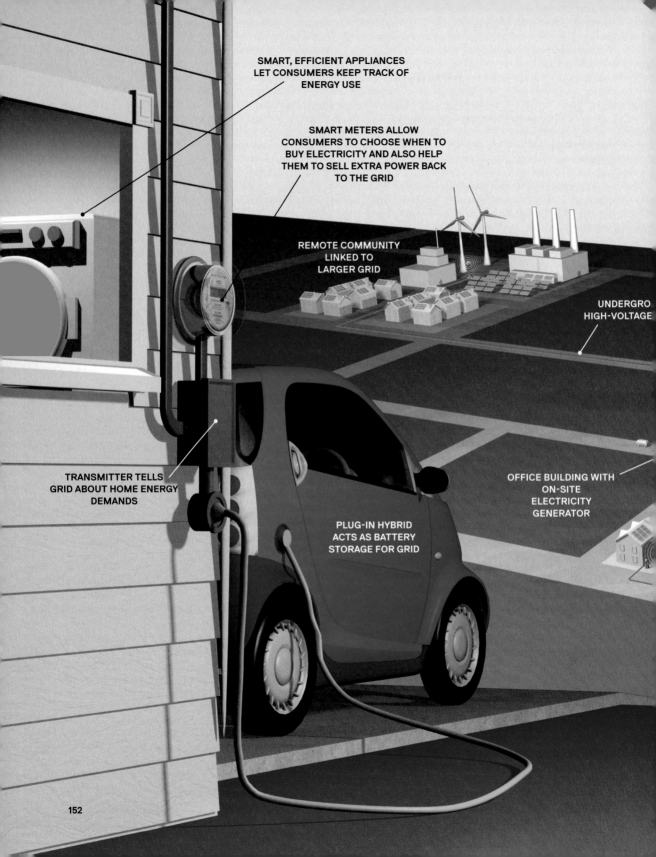

SMART, EFFICIENT APPLIANCES
LET CONSUMERS KEEP TRACK OF
ENERGY USE

SMART METERS ALLOW
CONSUMERS TO CHOOSE WHEN TO
BUY ELECTRICITY AND ALSO HELP
THEM TO SELL EXTRA POWER BACK
TO THE GRID

REMOTE COMMUNITY
LINKED TO
LARGER GRID

UNDERGRO
HIGH-VOLTAGE

TRANSMITTER TELLS
GRID ABOUT HOME ENERGY
DEMANDS

PLUG-IN HYBRID
ACTS AS BATTERY
STORAGE FOR GRID

OFFICE BUILDING WITH
ON-SITE
ELECTRICITY
GENERATOR

HOW A SUPER GRID WILL WORK

An electricity super grid with computer technology will make electricity use more efficient. It will be able to combine electricity from all sources—older power plants and new solar, wind, and geothermal plants. Computers will help the system adjust to different levels of demand during the day and avoid blackouts. They will also find trouble and fix it before blackouts can happen. Consumers will be able to make their own electricity, buy power when it's cheaper, and sell extra electricity back to the grid.

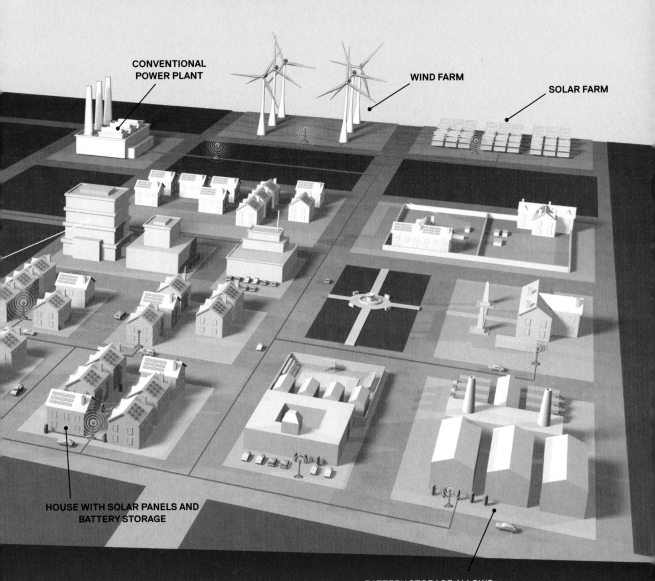

CONVENTIONAL POWER PLANT

WIND FARM

SOLAR FARM

HOUSE WITH SOLAR PANELS AND BATTERY STORAGE

BATTERY STORAGE ALLOWS CONSUMERS TO BUY POWER WHEN IT'S CHEAPER AND STORE IT FOR LATER USE

153

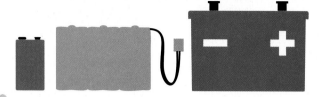

problem of meeting peak demand. Peak demand, like the demand caused by air conditioners on a hot day, happens for just a few hours a day. The really big peaks happen on just a few days a year. To be ready for peak demand, power companies keep gas- and coal-burning generators on standby. (You can't just turn a generator on and get power—it has to be warmed up first.) Those extra generators are burning fossil fuels, and putting CO_2 into the air, when they aren't even needed.

If we replaced these extra power plants with electricity storage, we could cut large amounts of CO_2 pollution and save money at the same time.

New types of batteries offer real promise in solving this problem. These are not the types of batteries you put in a flashlight, but very large ones that can store megawatts of power. (A medium-size coal-burning power plant puts out about 600 megawatts of power.) Hundreds of companies around the world are racing to produce larger, cheaper, more efficient batteries.

For example, a Japanese company now sells a room-size battery, called a *sodium-sulfur battery,* that can produce one megawatt of power for six hours. These are installed in groups. For example, six of these batteries together could produce six megawatts of power. Power companies use these batteries during peak hours of demand. They're very expensive, but using them is still much cheaper than running extra generators.

Unfortunately, the company that makes them can only produce a few batteries every year. But other companies are right behind. General Electric says it will soon have a battery that equals the one made in Japan. With growing competition and increased research, we can expect the cost of such large-scale batteries to fall.

CARS AS ENERGY STORAGE

To fight global warming, we need to replace hundreds of millions of gasoline-

This electric Tesla roadster can run for more than 200 miles when fully charged. Its battery can also be used as a storage system for electricity.

burning cars with electric cars. That will reduce CO_2 emissions—if the electricity does not come from fossil fuels. But to build all those cars, we need batteries that are powerful enough (and safe enough and small enough) to power automobiles. Automakers are working on those batteries right now.

One approach has been to adapt lithium ion batteries, the kind used in digital cameras and cell phones. Nissan, General Motors, and a small U.S. company called Tesla are all building cars with lithium ion batteries.

Once we have millions of electric cars, all of those millions of batteries will act as a giant electric storage system. Most of the batteries will be charged at

night, during off-peak hours (when the smart grid makes it cheaper). And once companies start making millions of car batteries, the price of batteries should come down even faster.

It should be possible to adapt that same technology for home use. One idea is to install large battery packs on city blocks, perhaps one for every four or five homes. The batteries could charge during off-peak hours (or when solar and wind power are producing) and then give off power at other times. One benefit would be to make homes more independent of the grid, in case of blackouts. It would also make it easier to store energy produced by local solar panels or wind turbines.

THE EUROPEAN AND NORTH AFRICAN SUPER GRID

A plan for a new electric super grid would link Europe and North Africa. The new grid will be able to collect clean solar energy in Africa and the Middle East and sell it throughout the region.

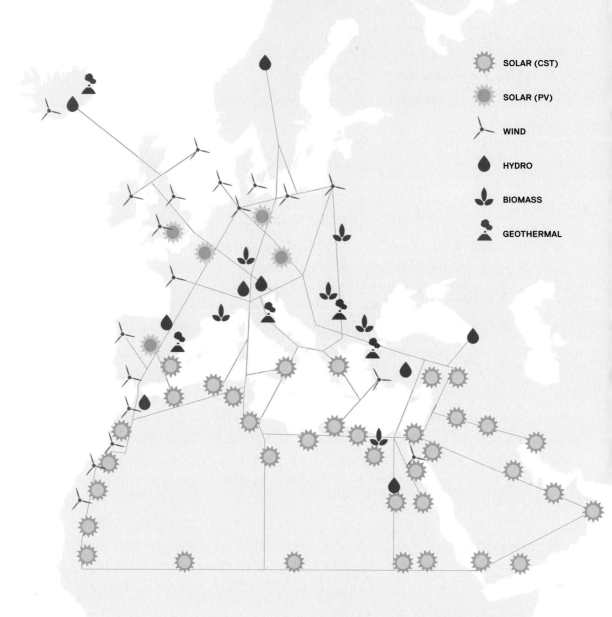

SOLAR (CST)

SOLAR (PV)

WIND

HYDRO

BIOMASS

GEOTHERMAL

DO-IT-YOURSELF ELECTRICITY

Twenty years ago, few people could predict how the personal computer, the cell phone, and the Internet would change the way we get and use information. In the same way, the smart grid will change the way we make and use energy. Instead of getting our electricity from a few large plants, we will get it from many different sources. Some of those sources might even be in our own backyards.

The smart grid will make it possible for electricity consumers to become producers. Rooftop photovoltaic panels, for example, make electricity whenever the sun is shining. Better batteries will make it possible to store some of that energy to use at night. A smart grid will make it easier to sell extra electricity back to the power company.

Right now, the number of rooftop photovoltaic panels is tiny, but in many areas the number is doubling every year. There is also growing interest in small home wind turbines in rural areas with a lot of space. Some experts predict that within 10 years, half of all households in the U.S. will be generating some of their own electricity.

A SUPER GRID

The technology to build a new smart grid already exists. And we have taken the first steps. In early 2009, President Barack Obama made developing a new electricity grid part of his economic stimulus bill.

Meanwhile, other countries are further along. China has already begun building a national smart grid that they say will be ready by the year 2020. There are also plans being drawn up for a super grid that would link Europe with North Africa and the Middle East. That would connect the cities of Europe with the wind and solar energy of those regions.

The United States must build a new national electric grid. Just by switching to a smart grid, we would save enough energy to cut CO_2 emissions by millions of metric tons a year. More important, it will make it possible to use all the renewable-energy sources we need to stop the climate crisis. The electric superhighway is ready to be built. We *can* build it—if we choose to.

Trash dumped on the tundra outside Ilulissat, Greenland.

CHAPTER 14

CHANGING THE WAY WE THINK

Before people act to stop the climate crisis, they must see that it is a danger right now.

Most people now understand that global warming is real and is caused by human action. Scientists have proven that the crisis threatens our very way of life. Yet, somehow, it's still hard to get people to make the choices that will stop the climate crisis.

Why is this so? Why is it hard to get people to take action to stop the climate crisis even *after* they know all the facts? It turns out that the human brain responds better to some dangers than to others.

159

We human beings are very good at responding to danger when it's right in front of us. But our brains are not very good at dealing with threats that seem far away.

Because we don't see global warming in front of us, we don't go into high alert. We don't act.

To stop global warming, we must find a way to get people to understand that there is a danger right now.

CHARGING RHINOS

Our nervous system evolved over millions of years to help us survive. It reacts very well to dangers like charging rhinos or deadly snakes. If we see a burning house or a car coming at us, our nervous system goes into high alert automatically. It can even learn to respond to modern threats, like losing a job and having no money. As long as we understand that the threat is real and is present now, we react. We don't need to think about it—we act.

But so far, the climate crisis has not seemed real to most people. The world's average temperature is rising now. But the difference is too small for some to notice. Looking at a graph of rising temperatures doesn't make us feel the danger.

The Arctic ice cap is melting right now, but it is far away. We don't see it every day. Even if we see a photo of a melting glacier, it doesn't seem dangerous to us.

Although the effects of global warming are happening now, the biggest problems will take place sometime in the future. There's no doubt that in the future, when young people today have grown up, the world will react. At that point, the damage of global warming will be all around. But by then it will be too late to stop it. We have to get people to act now. It will be easier if they understand that the threat is already here.

CAN YOU FEEL IT NOW?

As the climate crisis gets worse, people will begin to see the results around them. This is starting to happen now. We are beginning to experience weather we have not seen before, including heat waves, floods, and

A penguin on an iceberg in Antarctica. Many large ice sheets have already collapsed there, and West Antarctica is melting at a frightening rate.

HOW SMOKING BECAME UNCOOL

In the 1950s and early 1960s, when I was a kid, more than 40 percent of adult Americans smoked cigarettes. A lot of people thought smoking was a fun thing to do. Even if people didn't like smoking, they didn't think it was dangerous.

Then in 1964, the nation's chief doctor, the Surgeon General, put out a report that said that smoking led to cancer, heart disease, and other health problems. In 1966, the government said tobacco companies had to put a warning label on every pack of cigarettes. In 1969, the government banned cigarette advertising from television. Since then, the government has continued to educate people, especially young people, about the dangers of smoking.

In other words, the government acted to change the way people thought about smoking and to get them to change their habits. And it worked. Today, only about 20 percent of adult Americans smoke. Most people understand that smoking cigarettes causes lung cancer. Smoking in public is no longer welcome. And millions of people are healthier and live longer because they do not smoke. This happened even though the tobacco industry spent millions of dollars to deny that smoking causes disease.

This success story is a good lesson for the fight against global warming. If people can be persuaded to give up smoking, then surely they can be persuaded to give up fossil fuels.

U.S. SMOKING RATES

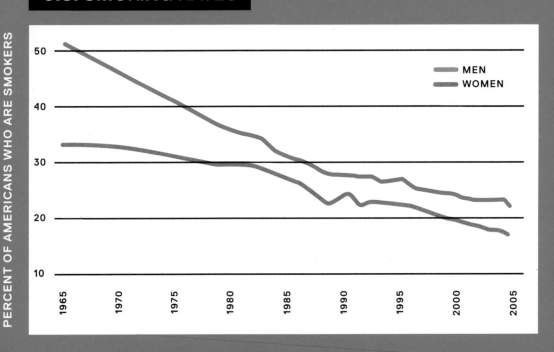

droughts. Giant storms, like Hurricane Katrina, are becoming more common. These storms are frightening evidence of the destruction that can be brought about by the climate crisis.

We are beginning to feel the effect of the crisis in other ways. In some areas, songbirds have vanished. Their migration patterns have been changed by global warming. The number of salmon off the coast of California is dropping. This is caused by a change in ocean currents and water temperature. These changes are helping to make people aware of the dangers of global warming.

But that's just the start.

If people are paying attention to the climate crisis today, will they keep paying attention?

We tend to have very short attention spans. And it's very hard to get people to change their habits. A crisis might make them change for a time, but it's very easy to slip back into old patterns.

You can see this every time the price of gas goes up. For a while, people rush to buy cars with better gas mileage. Then, when gas prices drop, they forget about the problem. They go back to buying cars with poor gas mileage. They stop thinking about electric cars or hybrids.

CHANGING MINDS

So to solve the climate crisis, we have to change the way we think. It won't be easy. The human race has never dealt with global warming before. We have no history lessons to prepare us. We don't have memories to warn us about the threat and make us want to act. This makes it even harder to get people to focus on the danger we face.

The good news is that human beings can work together for long-term goals. History is full of examples of communities and nations working together to solve problems. That ability is also in our brains.

Here are some of the things we must do to change the way we think:

▶ We have to appeal to people's deepest values. Every major religion says that humanity has a responsibility to protect and preserve the earth. That should be a powerful force to help us focus on the hard jobs we face. In the same way, most people feel a responsibility to future generations. We don't want to leave a ruined climate to the human beings who will come after us.

▶ We should resist being fearful. We want the world to wake up and see the danger of global warming. On the other hand, if people think the problem is hopeless, they will just give up. The danger is real, but we can still stop the worst effects of the climate crisis—if we act now.

▶ We have to get people to see the links between fighting global warming and solving the other problems we face. For example, building a new energy economy will create many new jobs.

▶ A natural human reaction to a problem is to look for one simple solution. However, there is not one simple solution to the climate crisis. We need to combine several different solutions at the same time. Some will work better than others, and we have to be okay with that, too.

None of this will be easy, but it can be done. Young people are especially open to new ideas and new ways of doing things. If we can get other people to change the way they think, even a little bit, we can get the world to act now, before it is too late.

Chartres Cathedral in France took more than a century to build, over several generations. This shows that people can learn to work together on a common long-term goal.

RELIGION AND THE ENVIRONMENT

All of the world's major religions say that humans should take
care of our Earth, as these quotations from some of them show:

ISLAM
**The world is beautiful and verdant, and verily God,
be He exalted, has made you His stewards in it, and
He sees how you acquit yourselves.**

TAOISM
**You should not burn [the vegetation of] uculti-
vated or cultivated fields, nor of mountains and
forests. You should not wantonly fell trees. You
should not throw poisonous substances into lakes,
rivers, and seas. You should not wantonly dig holes
in the ground and thereby destroy the earth.**

JUDAISM
**Do not dump waste in any place from which it could
be scattered by the wind or spread by flooding.**

HINDUISM
Do not cut trees because they remove pollution.

CHRISTIANITY
**God placed the human in the Garden of Eden to
serve and keep it.**

TOO MUCH STUFF

A lot of the information we get is in the form of ads. The average American now sees about 3,000 advertising messages per day. Those ads all say the same thing—buy more. And we've been listening. We are consuming more and more without thinking about what this is doing to our environment.

Sales of clothing in the United States doubled from 1991 to 2005. That's not because there were twice as many people. It's because we bought twice as many clothes. As we buy more, we waste more. In the U.S., we now produce 141 pounds of waste per day for every man, woman, and child in the nation.

You may have heard the saying "Money cannot buy happiness." It turns out this is true. Scientists have studied the happiness levels of people in different countries. They've found that once people have their basic needs met—food, shelter, clothing, health care—having more things does not make them happier. Yet, prodded by advertising, we continue to buy things as fast as we can.

To stop the climate crisis, we will all have to get used to the idea of consuming less and creating less waste. That doesn't mean we have to give up our standard of living. It just means spending less time and money trying to afford the latest sneakers (or cell phone or blue jeans). That's one way we can save the planet—and it might make us happier, too.

The average American supermarket, like this one in Portland, Oregon, carries more than 45,000 different items.

TOO MUCH INFORMATION

In the modern world, we have television, radio, the Internet, text messaging, Twitter, and a dozen other things to distract us. We are hit with a constant stream of news and noise. Much of the news we hear is bad news—crime, war, earthquakes, and other disasters. After a while, we tune it all out. In the middle of all this information, global warming can seem like just another headline. We listen, but we don't feel the need to do anything.

That's another habit we have to break—the habit of sitting back and doing nothing. Many people feel they can have no effect on what is going on in the world. If you believe you are powerless to stop the climate crisis, then it is pointless to even try. One way to get people to act is to show them what to do.

Everyone can be a leader in the fight against global warming.

People naturally want to cooperate with one another. If they see others leading the fight against the climate crisis, they will want to take part also.

Twenty years ago, almost no one in the United States recycled their trash. Today, most people do it without even thinking. How did this change happen? Concerned citizens started it. They recycled their own trash and then tried to get others to do so. After a while, towns and cities began passing recycling laws. Today, recycling is a habit for many people. It has become part of our daily life.

In the same way, we have to make fighting global warming a new habit. This is a big job. To stop the climate crisis, we must change the way the world thinks. This may be the most difficult thing we have to do. Yet our planet and future generations depend on it. Think about it.

The Amos Coal Power Plant in Raymond, West Virginia, produced more than 18 million tons of CO_2 emissions in 2006.

CHAPTER 15

THE TRUE COST OF CARBON

We must calculate the true cost of global warming and put a price on CO_2 pollution.

Carbon dioxide, the most significant source of global warming pollution, is invisible, tasteless, and odorless.

The true cost of carbon dioxide pollution is also invisible.

The next time you go by a gas station, look at the price of gasoline. That price includes what the oil companies paid for the petroleum. It includes the cost of turning it into gasoline and getting it to the gas station. The price also includes billions in profits for the oil companies.

But right now the price of gasoline (and other fossil fuels) does not include the cost of global warming. That includes damage to our crops and food supply, the destruction of our forests, and the flooding of coastal towns and cities. If you just look at global warming in terms of dollars and cents, the cost is enormous—*trillions* of dollars.

169

This neighborhood of new homes in Surrey, England, gets all of its electricity and heating from solar panels, passive solar design, and biomass.

tax should include cuts in other taxes so people would not suffer from the higher price of heating oil and gasoline.

I have been in favor of a CO_2 tax for some time. It is the simplest, most direct way of putting a price on carbon dioxide. It would immediately force businesses and consumers to start changing their habits. However, for some time now, Americans have been told that any new taxes are bad. Plus, coal and oil companies have spent millions of dollars on campaign contributions to congressmen. So it might be difficult to get such a tax through Congress.

2. Institute a cap and trade system, like the one used to cut SO_2 pollution. A plan to do this is at the heart of President Obama's climate bill. This bill aims to cut carbon dioxide emissions by 17 percent by the year 2020 and cut them 83 percent by 2050. Although these goals are smaller than those of other countries, it is still a giant step in the right direction.

In my opinion, the best solution would include both a CO_2 tax and a cap and trade system. Several countries, mostly in Europe, are already using both approaches.

3. Direct government regulation.
That means the government puts a limit on the amount of carbon dioxide you can release. This does not put a price on using carbon like a cap and trade system. Instead, it makes it against the law to emit too much CO_2 pollution. Along with cap and trade and a carbon tax, this is a very good idea. In 2009, the Environmental Protection Agency of the U.S. sent a plan to Congress to regulate carbon dioxide. We are waiting to see if Congress will approve the plan or if it will be stopped by the oil and coal industries.

4. Pass laws that force power companies to use renewable energy sources.
This has already been done in California and several other states. Thanks to these laws, there has been a surge of new investment for windmills and solar plants that would not have been built otherwise. If we can pass a national law, this surge in renewable-energy investment will grow rapidly. Other nations, including China and the nations of the European Union, have adopted this approach as well.

AN ECONOMIC OPPORTUNITY

Some people claim that carbon taxes or cap and trade systems will hurt our economy. Really, the opposite is true, as we saw with the Clean Air Act. If we don't change the way we do business, if we act like global warming isn't a real danger, then our economy will be in serious trouble. We will pay a price two ways: First, we will suffer the damage of the climate crisis. Second, we will lose out on a great opportunity.

That's right—the climate crisis is a danger, but it's also an opportunity. It's an opportunity to create new industries and new jobs. Businesses that build the technology for new energy sources will succeed. Countries that act now to end fossil fuel use will see their economies grow. I believe that renewable energy will be the engine of economic development for the next 25 years. It can create millions of jobs and save us from global warming at the same time.

But this will only happen if we change our economic thinking. We can't just be concerned with this year's profits. We have to look years into the future and plan for the new economy. We have to understand the real cost of pollution and the real value of our natural resources. And we have to be ready to act, today, to make the changes we need. Our future—and more important, our children's and grandchildren's future—depends on it.

Students rally for clean energy at the state capitol building in Lansing, Michigan.

CHAPTER 16

TAKING ACTION TOGETHER

Our government must act now to end the climate crisis.

We cannot end the climate crisis by acting only as individuals. The problem is too big and too global. We must work together, first as a nation and then with all the other nations of the world, to save our planet.

The only way to really have an impact on global warming is to get our country to act, and act in a big way. We need new rules and new laws that cut global warming pollution. We need government to spend money on renewable energy. We need policies that encourage renewable energy.

So far our government has been very slow to act. Almost every other country in the world has agreed to the Kyoto Protocol, an international treaty to reduce greenhouse gases. Of the industrialized nations, only the U.S. has not.

→ INCONVENIENT YOUTH

When Mary Doerr came to a training session for The Climate Project (TCP) in 2007, in many ways, she was like most people there. She wanted to learn about global warming, and she wanted to do something about it. However, at 16 years old, she was one of the youngest people who had ever attended one of these events.

TCP trains people around the world to educate other people by giving talks about the climate crisis. If you've seen the movie *An Inconvenient Truth*, you've seen me give one of these talks. Many people apply to go to these trainings, and they are usually adults. But that didn't stop Mary. As a teenager, she knew that global warming was, and continues to be, the most important issue facing her generation, and like a lot of young people, she wanted to do her part to help solve it.

Mary liked my talk, but she thought there was a better way to tell it for her age group. She and some friends rewrote the presentation to be shorter and to focus on how young people can get involved. And with some other teens, she formed a group called Inconvenient Youth (ICY).

Since then, ICY teen volunteers have been hard at work giving their versions of the talk to others teens across the country. In fall 2008, some members of the group went on tour with the band KSM. They visited 36 cities, reaching thousands of young people. Mary says that many of the kids she meets are "chomping at the bit" to get involved.

The ICY website is a social networking site where concerned teens can exchange ideas, advice, and tips. It can help you and your friends learn more about the dangers of the climate crisis and meet other young people who are concerned about it too. And it's a good place to look if you want to start taking action against the climate crisis in your school and community.

If you're like Mary and think global warming needs to be stopped, then isn't it time you became an Inconvenient Youth?

You can visit the Inconvenient Youth website at inconvenientyouth.org, and the Climate Project website at theclimateproject.org.

companies. No wonder it has been so hard to wake Americans up to the danger of global warming. Our own government has been misleading us.

THE PEOPLE'S VOICE

And yet, in spite of the massive attempt to hide or twist the truth, the American people today are waking up. Today, the great majority of Americans understand that global warming is real. Not only that, a 2009 ABC News/*Washington Post* poll showed that 75 percent believed the government should do something to regulate greenhouse gases.

One reason Americans have changed their minds is that environmental groups and concerned citizens have fought to get the truth out. They have organized to put pressure on Congress to act quickly to stop the threat. These organizations use many tools, including the Internet, to reach people with the facts.

In 2006, I founded one such organization: The Alliance for Climate Protection. Our goal is to build a solid majority of Republicans and Democrats who will support action against global warming. To date, we've mobilized more than two million people to work in their communities for action on the climate crisis. Thanks to the efforts of groups like the Alliance, both presidential candidates in 2008 supported cap and trade plans for carbon dioxide, one of the key steps we must take to slow the crisis.

But the fossil fuel lobby is still hard at work. Even in June 2009, as President Obama's Climate Bill was being voted on, some Republican representatives stood up in Congress and called global warming a lie. This shows us we cannot rest until our government has taken all the steps needed to turn things around.

To do this, we must harness the most powerful force in our democracy—the will of the American people. We must organize at the grass roots—in every town and community. That's the job of anyone who wants to be part of the global warming solution. Only then can we defeat the fossil fuel lobby. It will take a lot of work, but the truth is on our side.

History has shown that young people, even those too young to vote, can be a powerful force for change. You can help spread the truth about global warming. Just as important, you can help organize for the change we need. The information is in your hands now—it's up to you to make the choice.

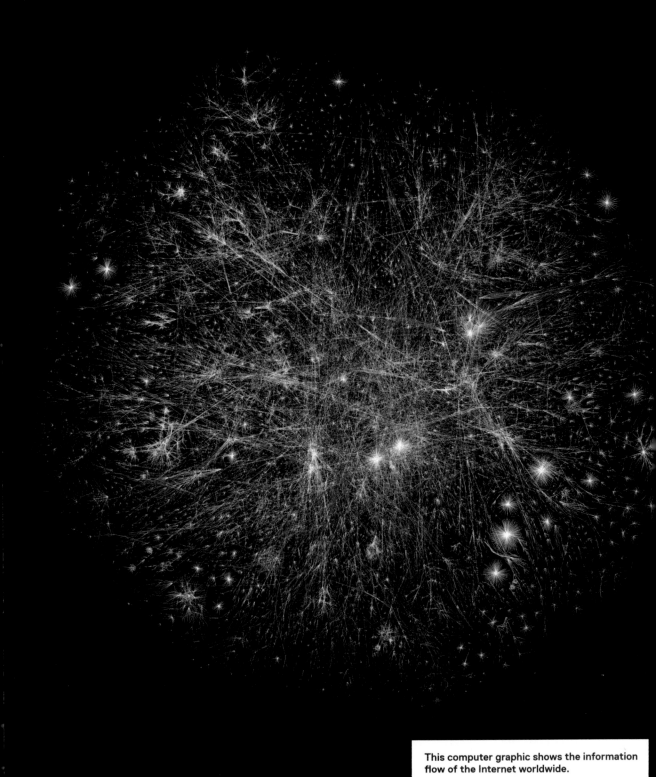

This computer graphic shows the information flow of the Internet worldwide.

THE POWER OF

INFORMATION

Information technology, including computers, software, and the Internet, can be an important tool in the fight against the climate crisis.

The climate crisis is a product of our modern way of life. We burn fossil fuels and create carbon dioxide to power our cars, our homes, and all sorts of technology. Luckily, some of that same modern technology can help us to reverse the climate crisis. Information technology can be one of the most powerful tools we have in the fight against global warming.

Computers can gather data from scientific instruments, even from satellites in space. That information will help us understand exactly how fast the climate is changing and what we can do to stop it. Software can help us to organize and display the facts in ways that are easy to understand. The Internet can help us to spread that information quickly to all parts

Information technology can also directly reduce global warming pollution by improving efficiency. Microchips can regulate energy use, and software can help design new types of renewable energy sources and make our old energy systems more efficient.

We can also use the Internet to organize the fight against global warming.

Thousands of environmental groups are using the Web to get out their message and reach supporters. Social networking sites like Facebook make it possible for activists to stay in touch and plan activities.

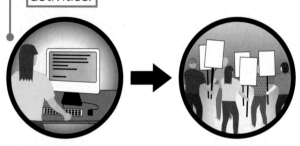

Information technology has transformed our lives. It has changed the way we communicate, learn, and relate to one another. Now we can use this technology to transform our lives another way—by ending our need for fossil fuels and saving our planet.

THE EARTH'S THERMOMETER

What if we had an exact measure of global warming? What if we knew exactly how much heat the atmosphere was trapping? It would be like taking the earth's temperature. That's just the kind of information that would move people to act faster to end the climate crisis.

But how can we take the earth's temperature? Is it even possible? Well, in fact, scientists came up with a plan to do exactly that—more than 10 years ago.

The plan was to put a satellite called Triana in orbit around the sun. The satellite would measure all of the heat from the sun that was hitting the earth. It would also measure all of the heat that was escaping from the earth. By subtracting the second number from the first, we would know exactly how much of the sun's energy was being trapped in our atmosphere. We would have a precise measurement of global warming. (The satellite would also give us a real-time TV image of the earth as it travels through space—kind of an earthcam.)

In 1998, Congress approved $250 million so NASA could build Triana. The satellite was built, and by 2001 it was ready to go into orbit. It had instruments for measuring global warming and a TV camera to transmit live video of the earth. It also had the ability to coordinate measurements of other satellites around the earth.

Triana was also given the job of replacing an older, smaller satellite that was already in position between the earth and the sun. The older satellite measures solar flares (large storms of energy on the surface of the sun that can damage electronic equipment like cell phone towers).

In 2009, Congress put aside money to take the satellite (now called DSCOVR) out of storage and get it ready for launch. NASA scientists have done this, but it is not clear when and if DSCOVR will go into space.

DSCOVR is probably the single most important piece of information technology we need to fight the climate crisis.

THE POWER OF A PICTURE

Sometimes the right information can change the way we look at the world. This famous photo, "Earthrise," is a good example. It was taken on December 24, 1968, by astronaut Bill Anders, during the Apollo 8 space mission. For most people, this photo was the first time we saw what our planet looked like from outer space.

We saw a beautiful, small blue sphere surrounded by the black vastness of space. The picture made many of us understand just how small our home is. We began to realize that the human race has to share this home, and we have to care for it so future generations can enjoy it.

This photo helped start the modern environmental movement, including the first Earth Day in 1970. Now it's up to us to find other images and other ways to spread the same message: we all must work together to save our home.

THE DEEP SPACE CLIMATE OBSERVATORY (DSCOVR)

When launched, DSCOVR will orbit the sun and remain directly betwe
earth and the sun at all times. That will give it a full-time view of the s
of our planet. The satellite will have a television camera so we will be a
live pictures of the earth from space. Other instruments on board will
the earth's albedo (see page 25), magnetic fields, and solar radiation.
will also help scientists to coordinate information from other satellites
the left of the earth, do you see the "L1" point? At that point, the gra
earth and the sun are exactly in balance. That will allow DSCOVR to s
position as it and the earth orbit the sun together.

SUN

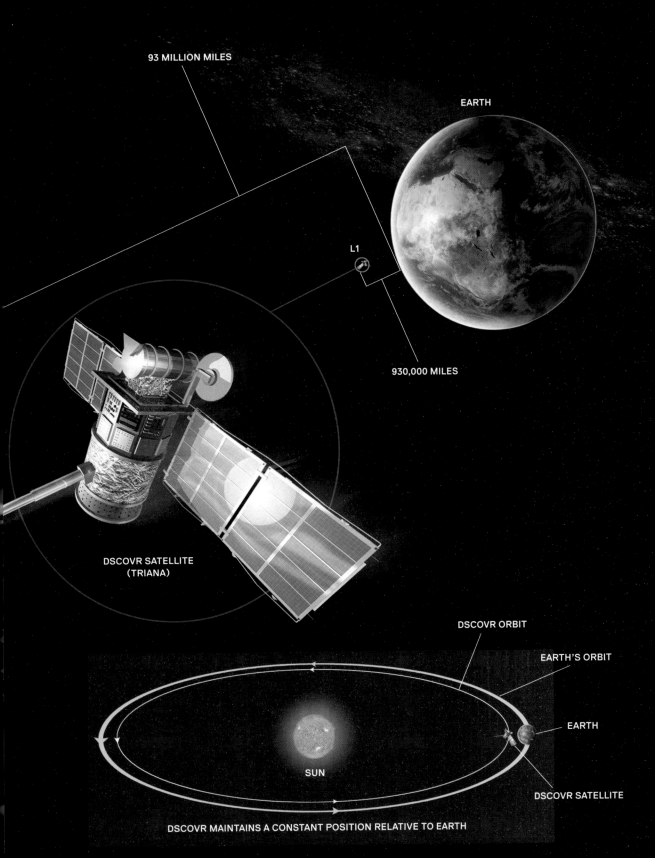

93 MILLION MILES

EARTH

L1

930,000 MILES

DSCOVR SATELLITE
(TRIANA)

DSCOVR ORBIT

EARTH'S ORBIT

EARTH

SUN

DSCOVR SATELLITE

DSCOVR MAINTAINS A CONSTANT POSITION RELATIVE TO EARTH

A CHANGING VIEW OF OUR CO_2

The Vulcan Project software lets us see how much carbon dioxide is coming from each county in the U.S. In this image, counties in red are creating the most carbon dioxide. The project is expanding to create maps of every nation in the world.

0.0—0.2
0.2—0.5
0.5—1.0
1.0—2.0
2.0—3.5
3.5—6.5
6.5—15.5
15.5—8,000

KILOTONS (1,000 TONS) OF CARBON EMISSIONS PER YEAR

CAN YOU SEE THE WARMING?

The satellite DSCOVR, if it is finally launched, will give us a dramatic way of showing that global warming is happening. But technology can give us other ways of "seeing" global warming, even without a satellite.

At Purdue University, a group of scientists have developed a software program called Vulcan (named after the Roman god of fire). Vulcan makes it possible to see the amount of CO_2 emissions from any spot in North America—and soon from everywhere in the world.

The same Purdue team developed another computer tool called Hestia (named after the Greek goddess of the home). Hestia displays maps that show how much heat energy is wasted in cities and towns. If you look at a Hestia map of an area, you can see which buildings are leaking the most heat. With tools like Vulcan and Hestia, we can help people to finally "see" global warming.

MAKING US MORE EFFICIENT

Information technology can do more than gather and display information. It can directly reduce CO_2 emissions by making machines more efficient. All sorts of appliances and machines are now being run by tiny computers on microchips. For example, industrial motors often run at a constant rate even when they are not working. A microchip in a motor can adjust the motor speed to match the workload. That can save large amounts of energy that would otherwise be wasted.

In the same way, electronic sensors and microchips can adjust electric lights to turn them down when there is more natural light from the outside. Computer systems in buildings can save money on heating and air-conditioning. They can also find places where heat is leaking from walls, windows, or heating systems.

Computers can also make businesses more efficient. If you run a shipping company, you make money by delivering freight. But what happens when your truck makes a delivery and has to come back empty? Every time you have to drive an empty truck across the country, you lose money and you waste energy.

In 2007, about 25 percent of all truck trips in the U.S. were made by empty trucks. Today, some freight companies are using computer systems to match trucks with deliveries and cut down on waste. Of course, this also cuts down on carbon emissions.

Communicating over the Internet or by text message is actually more energy efficient than older ways of communicating. For example, it takes less energy to send the news to you on a web page than to deliver a thick newspaper to your door. E-mail uses less energy than old-fashioned snail mail. However, we still need to make this new technology more energy efficient. Right now, about 2 percent of all global warming pollution

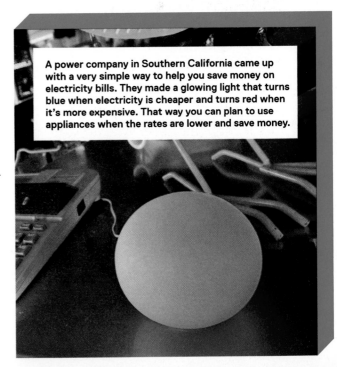

A power company in Southern California came up with a very simple way to help you save money on electricity bills. They made a glowing light that turns blue when electricity is cheaper and turns red when it's more expensive. That way you can plan to use appliances when the rates are lower and save money.

comes from information technology. Computer networks, including the Internet, are poorly designed and waste energy. Computers, monitors, printers, and many other devices must be redesigned to use less electricity.

A TOOL FOR ORGANIZING

We cannot solve this crisis without global collective action. The Internet is the perfect platform for making this happen. Young people don't have to be told that technology has changed the way we connect with one another. Text messaging, Twitter, Facebook, and YouTube are just a few examples of how we use electronic devices to connect with one another. Now environmental activists are using these powerful tools to organize public support to fight the climate crisis.

There may be as many as two million environmental groups that are using the Internet to get their message out. Some of these organizations, like The Alliance for Climate Protection (see p. 187) have

Hurricane Katrina
August 29, 2005

Photo: NOAA

New computer software made my global warming presentation better, easier to update, and more effective.

millions of members. Some are small and local. They are working not just to stop the climate crisis but also to protect the environment, end pollution, and work for equality and fairness in society. It may be the largest social movement in all of human history. It's hard to imagine that this would have been possible without our new Internet-based tools.

Sometimes, just getting information to the public is enough to make change happen. U.S. law now forces businesses to publish information about the amount of air pollution they create. Once that happened, newspapers, television, and radio began to list the worst polluters in every area. Companies did not want to be on that list, so they began, by themselves, to cut their pollution.

NEW TECHNOLOGY FOR A NEW GENERATION

When I first gave the talk that became *An Inconvenient Truth,* I used an old-fashioned slide projector. I remember what a difference it made when I transferred my slideshow to a computer-based presentation. Not only did it make it easier to add new information, I found my performance was better and audiences enjoyed the talk more.

I have now trained more than 3,000 people in dozens of countries to give updated talks. They are organized through The Climate Project, and we stay in touch through the Internet. We can create new slides and send them out electronically to everyone in the world who is giving the same talk. This means we can respond to new developments and get important information out much more quickly.

Technology like that was not around when I was growing up. Like everyone else in my generation, I've had to learn to use it. I've also come to see the power that this technology has to help us in the fight against the climate crisis.

Another thing I've learned is that young people, who have grown up with this technology, are often the best at finding new ways to use it.

So here's a challenge I am giving you. Let's find a thousand new ways to use information technology to help us stop global warming. We know the facts are on our side. It's up to us to make sure we gather information, organize it, and get it out to the public. If we do, we will be able to keep building our movement and turn the tide against global warming.

CONCLUSION

OUR CHOICE

Like anyone, I sometimes wish that I could go back in time and change mistakes I've made. I wish I could take back something I said or change something I did.

It's easy when you look back to see what you did wrong and what you would do differently. Sadly, we can't travel back in time and make different choices. None of us has the power to change the past.

But all of us have the power to change the future.

The choices we make now will decide what the world will look like 20 or 30 years from now. Twenty years from now, if I'm still alive, I'll be an old man. But you'll be a young adult.

Can you imagine your children asking you about the climate crisis? Can you imagine them asking, "What happened when the ice caps started melting? What did people do when they learned about global warming? What did they do to save the planet?"

Two streams meet in the jungle of Costa Rica.

A TIME FOR HOPE

I hope you don't have to say to them, "Instead of acting, people argued. They didn't want to believe the scientists. Some politicians said the whole thing was a fake. Some corporations were making a lot of money from fossil fuels, and they opposed any change. The world just couldn't agree about what to do."

Instead, I hope you'll be able to say this: "When I was a kid, I was worried about global warming, but in 2009 things started to change. We had a new president who understood that the climate crisis was very serious. People began to accept the fact that the crisis was real. They saw clues in the changing weather and melting glaciers. They started demanding an end to the burning of fossil fuels. Even people who had fought against change began to switch sides. That was the year the people of the world finally began to act to save our home, planet Earth."

I know that a lot of the information in this book can be frightening. But I still have hope that the world can come together to end the climate crisis, and I really believe it will—when all of us insist on it. I hope that when you're an adult, you'll be able to tell the great story of how you saw the world change for the better. I hope the story you tell will be something like this:

A TIME OF CHANGE

In 2009, after years of delay, the United States finally began to lead the world in fighting global warming. Congress passed a law to cut carbon dioxide pollution. This law made it expensive to put more CO_2 into the air, so the polluters stopped doing it so much. At the same time, the government put money into renewable energy like solar, wind, and geothermal. And thanks to those actions, our country began to change its energy habits.

It wasn't just energy that changed. We changed the way we grew our food. We changed our factories and businesses.

We changed the way we traveled and the way we built our homes. We planted millions of trees. At first it was the cost of carbon that drove the change, but soon, when people saw the benefits of renewable energy, they wanted to change even more.

That same year, in December, all the nations of the world gathered in Copenhagen, Denmark. The representatives did something that many thought was impossible. They wrote a new treaty to unite the world in stopping the climate crisis. It was just the beginning, and many other steps had to be taken. But that first step showed the way forward.

It turned out that most nations of the world came to understand that they had to do something. Nations like China and the United States, which produced the most carbon dioxide, helped lead the way. Rich nations and poor nations agreed to work together. Countries like Brazil and Indonesia agreed to stop the cutting of rain forests. Japan and the nations of Europe shared ideas they had developed to cut carbon emissions.

The governments acted because the people of the world demanded it. Hundreds of thousands, then millions of grassroots groups grew up. These groups connected with one another, using the Internet, and formed a powerful alliance that pushed for global change.

In order to fight the climate crisis, these groups had to push for other changes. They demanded worldwide reforms in education and health care and made sure girls had an equal chance to go to school. They challenged corruption in government and fought for democratic reforms. They demanded reform in agriculture, which helped spread organic farming. And they made sure that the new

President Obama spoke about new energy technology as an important part of our future economy at Nellis Air Force Base in May 2009.

energy systems helped lift people out of poverty.

We didn't know it then, but 2009 was the turning point. It was the start of some of the biggest changes the world has ever seen. Instead of global warming, we saw changes in government, business, education, farming, and every other part of our lives. Most of all, we changed the way we thought about the planet. The people of the world came to understand that it was our job to protect the earth. We no longer accepted old habits that were leading to its destruction.

A TIME FOR YOUTH

As I said, I hope that's the story you get to tell. I know that these changes are possible. Whether it happens like that or not depends on what we do right now.

It may seem that as a young person, there is nothing you can do to help. Young people do not vote or write laws. You can't decide to buy an electric car or to insulate your home. So what can young people do?

Young people can lead the way. To stop the climate crisis, we have to change the world. And we cannot change the world without the help of young people.

Young people are not afraid of change. You are often the first to take up new ideas and to spread them. You aren't afraid to challenge old habits, to be creative, to dream up better ways of doing things. Young people know that it's possible to make the world a better place.

Time and again, young people have invented new technologies or come up with new ideas that have changed the world. I remember in 1969 when the first man landed on the moon. All of the systems engineers at NASA raised their arms and cheered with joy. Their average age was 26 years old.

That means that a lot of those young engineers were teenagers when the moon mission was first announced. They were young people who became inspired and excited about space exploration. They decided to make a difference and to take part in the great adventure of space travel.

Now we are trying to get the human race to start on another great adventure. It's not a trip to outer space, but a mission to save our Earth. And we need young people to become part of that mission.

It's up to you to decide how you will take part. Will you help invent a new kind of solar energy or a new type of electric car? Or will you become an activist and organize for change? Maybe you'll dedicate your life to saving the rain forest or organic farming or ending poverty. Or maybe you'll lead just by getting your family to change its habits and become more energy aware.

I've already seen the energy and passion of so many young people around the world who are meeting this challenge. For them, it is simply unthinkable that we should fail. And I believe that because of you, we won't.

A young activist plays guitar at the Camp for Climate Action in Blackheath, England.

There is no question that the human race can meet the challenge of the climate crisis—if we act in time.

We have everything we need to meet this challenge. We have the scientific knowledge and the technology. More important, we have the examples of history—times in the past when people faced great dangers, whether it was a world war or a worldwide economic crisis. In the past, when things looked the worst, people pulled together and found solutions. That's what we must do now.

We should know what we're up against. Global warming *is* a threat. But at the same time, we should be excited about the possibilities before us. The climate crisis is a threat, but it's also a great opportunity. We are at an important moment in human history. If we choose the right path, we will be able to change our world for the better.

If we act now, then I know in the future you and your children and grandchildren will be able to look around and see a beautiful world. You'll see a world that's in balance with nature, where fewer people live in poverty, and where the future looks bright. That's why, in spite of everything, I have hope today, and I think you should, too.

When you look at it from space, our beautiful planet is like the Garden of Eden. It belongs to all humankind, both living and yet to be born. Today we have the power to destroy that garden, but we also have the power to save it.

IT'S OUR CHOICE.

LET'S MAKE THE
RIGHT ONE.

ACKNOWLEDGMENTS

I am grateful first of all to my wife, Tipper, for her support and encouragement; my children, Karenna, Kristin, Sarah, and Albert; my brother-in-law, Frank Hunger; and my entire family for their encouragement, assistance, and love.

A special thanks at the outset to my two outstanding research assistants, Brad Hall and Jordan Pietzsch, for doing a truly extraordinary job in tracking down, assessing, and verifying thousands of facts, figures, quotations, studies, and analyses that have been essential for this book. Under the direction of Kalee Kreider, who has been of invaluable assistance in all of my climate work, they also organized on my behalf most of the more than 30 "Solutions Summits" over the past three years. In this respect, they took over the excellent work of Elliot Tarloff, who organized the first wave of Solutions Summits and also did voluminous research. One of my two research assistants on *The Assault on Reason*, Elliot generously stayed another year, delaying his entrance to law school to begin the research for me on this project. Roy Neel has ably managed the entire staff here in Nashville to provide sustained support for all aspects of this project, even as the staff continued to handle the rest of their ongoing work. Beth Prichard Alpert has made the trains run on time and has coordinated all of the telephone calls and meetings for this project over the past few years. Her role as my Deputy Chief of Staff is indispensable. Conor Grew has also been indispensable and indefatigable in helping me in multiple ways—especially on the road. Lisa Berg and Patrick Hamilton have also played important supportive roles, as have Elizabeth Spencer, Bill Huskey, Anna Katherine Owen, and every other member of the staff. And a special thanks to Dwayne Kemp for his culinary mastery—including on most Saturdays and Sundays as the work on this project intensified over the past year.

I am especially grateful to the many distinguished scientists and engineers who participated in the Solutions Summits and who, in most cases, continued to remain involved in the project by sending new material, research findings, papers in the final stages of review prior to publication, and answers to questions that came up after the sessions in which they participated. Their insights and explanations really make up the heart of this book. I would like to thank them all individually by name; because of space constraints, I have done so on the book's website, www.ourchoicethebook.com.

I want to thank The Alliance for Climate Protection, headed by Maggie Fox (and headed by Cathy Zoi when this project began), for all of their help in sponsoring the Solutions Summits and in providing additional research help. I am proud to donate all of my earnings from this book to the Alliance, as I did with *An Inconvenient Truth*. I also want to thank my partners at Generation Investment Management for their generous help in reviewing the outline for the book at the beginning, reading selected chapters for factual accuracy, and reading the entire manuscript toward the end.

Similarly, my partners at Kleiner Perkins Caulfield & Byers (KPCB) have been of invaluable assistance in reviewing the outline and helping with the answers to detailed questions. Both Generation and KPCB have attended all of the Solutions Summits and have recruited CEOs and business leaders to join the scientists, engineers, and technology and policy experts in ensuring that the in-depth discussions benefited from their commercial and market insights and experience.

For purposes of full disclosure, some of the information that I gathered for this book outside of the Summits also resulted from my affiliations with The Alliance for Climate Protection, Generation Investment Management, and Kleiner Perkins Caufield & Byers. As an advocate and a businessman, I also invest in alternative energy companies.

I would like to thank Eileen Kreit, Publisher of Puffin Books, and Kristin Gilson, Editorial Director. Thanks also to Gerard Mancini, Associate Publisher, Puffin Books and Viking Children's Books; Jen Haller, Associate Publisher, Penguin Young Readers Group; Don Weisberg, President, Penguin Young Readers Book; Shanta Newlin, Publicity Director; Felicia Frazier, Sales Director; and the Penguin Young Readers Group sales and marketing teams.

I want to thank my friend Steve Murphy, former CEO of Rodale, and Maria Rodale, CEO and Chairman of Rodale, for their belief in and commitment to *Our Choice*, and for all of the wonderful help Rodale has provided all along the way. I am especially grateful to my outstanding editor for the adult edition, Karen Rinaldi, who is also Senior Vice President, General Manager, and Publisher at Rodale, for her skill, dedication, and stamina—and for crucially important suggestions about the best way to present this material.

Special thanks to Richie Chevat, the very talented writer who "translated" my text into language accessible to young readers aged 8 to 14; and to the book's designers, Hjalti Karlsson and Jan Wilker of karlssonwilker. I am also grateful to Liz Lomax, who did the clay models of the earth on the front and back covers.

I have once again enjoyed the chance to work with my friend Charles Melcher, who is the very best at book architecture, design, and production. It is difficult to adequately thank the men and women at Melcher Media who put in so many long hours—day and night—on the pictures, graphics, and related work, including: Kurt Andrews; Erin Barnes; Duncan Bock; David E. Brown; Dennis Bunnell; Amélie Cherlin; Daniel del Valle; Cheryl Della Pietra; Max Dickstein; Bonnie Eldon; Alissa Faden; Marilyn Fu; Sallie Gmeiner; Barbara Gogan; Filomena Guzzardi; Stephanie Heimann; Coco Joly; Terry Klockow; Phil MacDonald; Lisa Maione; Marie Mulcahy; Lauren Nathan; Brian Payne, Sr.; Richard Petrucci; Lia Ronnen; Holly Rothman; Jessi Rymill; Lindsey Stanberry; Shoshana Thaler; Scott Travers; Rebecca Wiener; Lee Wilcox; and Megan Worman.

Don Foley, in my opinion the best graphic artist in the world for this kind of material, has been skillful in creating the illustrations—and patient in modifying them through multiple iterations to align the details and conceptual proportions to the best available science and research. Thank you for a terrific job, Don! Charles Melcher and his team served up a rich menu of pictures from which to choose, and others offered suggestions for particular images. I am grateful to all of the photographers whose work appears in this book. I particularly want to thank my friend Yann Arthus-Bertrand, for generously providing several images from his spectacular body of work. In addition, I am once again grateful to National Geographic for donating the use of several of their wonderful photographs for this book. And thanks to Tom Mangelsen for his photo of penguins that opens the Introduction.

I want to thank my friend Natilee Duning for once again volunteering her time to line edit many of my rough chapter drafts; my friend and partner Joel Hyatt and my friend Mike Feldman for important advice; and my agent and friend, Andrew Wylie, for his advice and for once again skillfully working out the various arrangements crucial to this book's publication.

PHOTO AND ILLUSTRATION CREDITS

The author wishes to recognize the following individuals and companies for generously supporting The Alliance for Climate Protection by contributing photographs to this project:

The Associated Press; Argos Collectif; Yann Arthus-Bertrand; Aurora Photos; Edward Burtynsky; Robert Clark; Livia Corona; Hélène David; Envision Stock Photography; Mitch Epstein; Getty Images; Robert W. Ginn; Chris Jordan; Vince LaForet; Tony Law; Len Jenshel and Diane Cook; Alex S. MacLean; Magnum Photos, Tom Mangelsen, Sean Nolan; the National Geographic Society and its photographers—Jonathan Blair, Michael Melford, George F. Mobley, James C. Richardson, Tyrone Turner, Willis D. Vaughn; the *Los Angeles Times*; the *Syracuse Post-Dispatch*; OnAsia Images; Panos Pictures; Peter Arnold Inc.; Redux Images; Sipa Press; George Steinmetz; UNICEF; and Zuma Press.

Images are referenced by page number. All photographs and illustrations are copyright © by their respective sources.

7: NASA; 9: Tom Mangelsen; 11: Noah Seelam/AFP/Getty Images; 13: Sean Nolan/seannolan.com; 14: Ralph Orlowski/Getty Images; 24: Topham/The Image Works; 28: Ian Berry/Magnum Photos; 38: Martin Bond/Still Pictures/Peter Arnold Inc.; 40: Naturimages; 44: James C. Richardson/National Geographic Stock; 46: Courtesy Barley & Pfeiffer Architects; 48: Leah Nash/*The New York Times*/Redux; 52: Frank Huster/Aurora Photos; 55: Paul Langrock/Zenit/Laif/Redux; 56: courtesy Tom Rielly/ted.com; 58: Palmi Gudmundson/Nordic Photos/Aurora Photos; 63: Newscom; 68: Nelson Almeida/Getty Images; 73: Chris Knapton/SPL/Photo Researchers; 74: Paulo Fridman/Polaris; 76: Dr. Rob Stepnewy/SPL/Photo Researchers; 77: Pornchai Kittiwongsakul/AFP/Getty Images; 78: Mike Derer/Associated Press; 79: Paul Langrock/Zenit/Laif/Redux; 80: Øyvind Hagen/StatoilHydro; 82: Jim Olive/Peter Arnold Inc.; 83: Paul Corbit Brown; 86–87: Christoph Busse/Peter Arnold Inc.; 88: Edward Burtynsky courtesy Hasted Hunt Kraeutler, New York/Nicholas Metivier Gallery, Toronto; 90: Peter Essick/Aurora Photos; 92: Peter Essick/Aurora Photos; 94: Sergei Supinsky/AFP/Newscom; 98: Yann Arthus-Bertrand/Altitude; 101: Eduardo Martino/Panos Pictures; 102: Vinai Dithajohn/OnAsia.com; 103: Jay Ullal/Courtesy of Orangutan Outreach, redapes.org; 105: Guenter Fischer/The World of Stock; 108: Vince LaForet; 109: Gianluigia Guercia/Getty Images; 110: Adrian Bradshaw/Liason/Getty Images; 112: James C. Richardson/National Geographic Stock; 116–117: James C. Richardson/National Geographic Stock; 118: Arthur Rothstein/Library of Congress; 120: Brian Vander Brug/

The Los Angeles Times; 121: Steve Satushek/Getty Images; 122: Jeff Hutchens/Getty Images; 124: George Osod/Panos; 128–129 (left to right): Asad Zaidi/UNICEF; Lynsey Addario/VII; Giacomo Pirozzi/UNICEF; Richard Lord/The Image Works; 131: Stuart Freedman/Panos; 132: Abbas/Magnum Photos; 134: Courtesy of Siemens AG, Energy Sector; 137: Ullstein-Unkel/Peter Arnold Inc.; 139: Chris Jordan; 140: Al Golub/Associated Press; 142: Philip Hall/Sipa Press; 143: Tyrone Turner/National Geographic Stock; 145: Rony Zakaria/OnAsia.com; 146: Mark Ralston/AFP/Getty Images; 148: Kevin Moloney/*The New York Times*/Redux; 149: Jeff Jacobson/Redux; 151: Courtesy of Cook+Fox Architects; 155: Courtesy of Tesla; 158: Ashley Cooper/GHG Photos/Aurora Photos; 161: Yann Arthus-Bertrand/Altitude; 164: TIPS Images; 166: Lyza Danger Gardner; 168: Mitch Epstein; 170: Andrew Kornylak/Aurora Photos; 173: Joe Raedle/Getty Images; 174: Wade Payne/AP Photo; 175: Riccardo Venturi/Contrasto/Redux; 176: Raf Madka/View/Artedia; 178: Jim West/The Image Works; 181: Frank Augstein/AP Photo; 185: Ericka Ekstrom; 186: Court Mast on behalf of Inconvenient Youth; 188: Bell Labs/Lumeta Corp; 191: NASA; 194: The Vulcan Project/Dr. Kevin Gureny and Purdue University; 195: Eugene Garcia/*The Orange County Register*/Zuma Press; 196: Courtesy Eric Lee/Paramount Classics; 199: Jon Holloway/Stock Connection/Aurora Photos; 201: Isaac Brekken/Associated Press; 202: Oli Scarff/Getty Images; 203: Andrea Gjestvang/MOMENT.

Illustrations on pages 20–21, 32–33, 43, 45, 53, 65, 72, 85, 93, 115, 141, 152–153, and 192–193 © 2009 by Don Foley.

Illustration on page 22 © Tom Van Sant/GeoSphere Project and Michael Fornalski; illustration on page 25 © Michael Fornalski.

Infographics on pages 18, 46, 51 (top), 60, 61, 64, 66, 75, 95, 100, 126–127, 130, 136, 138, 156, 162, 171, 182, and 194 by mgmt. design.

INFOGRAPHIC SOURCES

18: Drew T. Shindell, et al., *Science*, in press, 2009; 34: Benjamin K. Sovacool, *Energy Policy* 36, 2008; 51: American Wind Energy Association; National Renewable Energy Laboratory; 61: National Oceanic and Atmospheric Administration; Jonathan T. Hagstrum, *Earth and Planetary Science Letters* 236, 2005; 64: Massachusetts Institute of Technology, *The Future of Geothermal Energy*, 2006; 75: Ethanol: North Carolina Cooperative Extension Service, October 2007; biodiesel: National Sustainable Agriculture Information Service; 95: World Nuclear Association; Federation of American Scientists; 96: U.S. Department of Energy; 100: United Nations Food and Agriculture Organization, *State of the World's Forests* 2007; 106–107: David Raup and John Seposki, *Science*, March 19, 1982; 126–127: U.S. Census; United Nations Population Division, *World Population* to 2300, 2004; Carbon Dioxide Information Analysis Center; *AAAS Atlas of Population and Environment*; 130: United Nations Population Division; CIA World Factbook; 138: Philips; U.S. Department of Energy; 156: DESERTEC Foundation; 162: U.S. Centers for Disease Control and Prevention; 171: Patterson Clark, *The Washington Post*, February 26, 2009; 182: Pew Research Center for People & the Press, "A Deeper Partisan Divide Over Global Warming"

I have worked to ensure that this book contributes as little as possible to our greenhouse gases and, indeed, represents some of the actions we can take to lessen our impact on the atmosphere.

The North American editions of *Our Choice* are printed on a 100 percent recycled paper that was custom-made for this book by Newton Falls Fine Paper in Newton Falls, New York. It contains 10 percent post-consumer waste, with the balance coming from industrial waste streams. Both sources of pulp recycle paper that might otherwise go into landfills. Compared with paper made of virgin fiber, the stock used in *Our Choice* conserved 1,153 trees and reduced greenhouse gas emissions by about 110,000 pounds of CO_2. This also saved 366 million BTUs of energy and reduced wastewater by 528,000 gallons. By using a lighter 68-pound paper, rather than the standard 80-pound thickness, an additional 15 percent of paper fiber, CO_2 emissions, energy, and water was saved.

This book was printed and bound by World Color in Taunton, Massachusetts. The printer was chosen, in part, because of its proximity to the paper mill and the publisher's warehouse, thus minimizing the amount of fuel used in shipping and the related CO_2 emissions.

Our Choice is a CarbonNeutral publication. The carbon emissions that resulted from the manufacturing of this book were calculated by the CarbonNeutral Company. For every ton of CO_2 produced, the CarbonNeutral Company has arranged for a ton of CO_2 to be saved by climate-friendly projects.

In order to avoid the destruction of our forests, it is important that we use paper pulp sources that are responsibly managed and sustainable. For this reason, I have made sure that all of the suppliers I worked with on this project, the paper company, the printer, the publisher, Penguin Group (USA), even the book producer, Melcher Media, have demonstrated their commitment to sustainable forestry practices by gaining certification from the Forestry Stewardship Council (FSC) and/or working with FSC certified companies. This book is FSC certified.

The next step in reducing this book's effects on the environment is yours. When you're finished reading *Our Choice*, please don't throw it away; rather, pass it along to a friend, to a library, or to someone who you feel needs to read it.

CERTIFIED CARBON NEUTRAL® Publication

CarbonNeutral.com
CO_2 emissions reduced to net zero in accordance with The CarbonNeutral Protocol

© **Mixed Sources**
Product group from well-managed forests, controlled sources and recycled wood or fibre
www.fsc.org Cert no. BV-COC-031730
© 1996 Forest Stewardship Council

FSC